The Official Study Guide for the Pleasure Craft Operator Card

This boating safety course manual has been approved by Transport Canada strictly on the basis that it meets the minimum requirements of basic boating safety knowledge set out in Transport Canada's Boating Safety Course and Test Syllabus. (TP 14932 E) For more information visit us online at **www.BOATERexam.com**

Skipper Online Services (SOS) Inc.
o/a *BOATERexam.com*®
203-1568 Carling Ave
Ottawa, ON K1Z 7M4
Tel: 1-866-688-2628

info@boaterexam.com
www.BOATERexam.com

Second Edition, 2012

***BOATERexam.com*®**
is a proud member of the
Canadian Safe Boating Council

Printed in Canada
Written by Skipper Online Services (S.O.S.) Inc.

PLEASURE CRAFT OPERATOR CARD (PCOC)

A PCOC is issued upon successfully completing a Transport Canada Safe Boating Exam. The card is good for life and there are no annual fees.

DO YOU NEED A PCOC*?

If you operate any recreational powered watercraft, you require a PCOC*. The law applies to all operators regardless of their age, the size of the engine or the length of the watercraft. This also includes electric trolling motors and sailboats fitted with engines. There are no age restrictions to become certified and the PCOC is good for life. Failure to carry a PCOC* can result in fines administered by any officer of the peace.

**Or proof of competency*

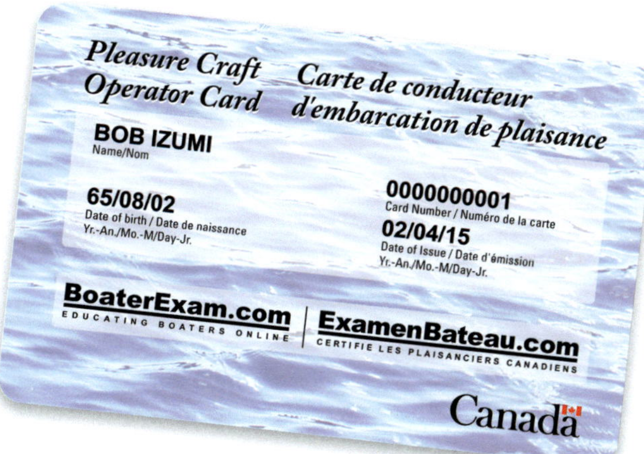

WHERE TO GET A PCOC?

BOATERexam.com® offers 2 convenient options to get certified:

❶ Online Course

Our online course is the most convenient way to get certified, since it allows you to study from home at your own pace. Once you have completed and passed the final exam, you can print a temporary card immediately. Your permanent card will arrive in the mail within 3-4 weeks. The official course for BOATERexam.com® is available online at www.BOATERexam.com, 24hrs a day.

❷ Testing Locations

Look for BOATERexam.com at tradeshows such as boat & sportsmen shows across Canada and take your *boater exam*® on the spot. BOATERexam.com also has boating safety teams that offer on-site certification at key retail partners coast-to-coast. Look for the Official BOATERexam.com blue tents in your community.

For a complete listing of upcoming events and official exam centres, visit **www.BOATERexam.com**

For more information, please contact our friendly customer service centre, open seven days a week.

Call toll-free at **1-866-688-2628** *or* log on to **www.BOATERexam.com**

BOATERexam.com® is a Transport Canada approved course provider and is the largest provider of Pleasure Craft Operator Cards in the country.

1. THE BOAT

2. BOATING EQUIPMENT

3. MINIMUM REQUIRED SAFETY EQUIPMENT

4. TRIP PLANNING

5. EMERGENCY PREPAREDNESS

6. SAFE BOAT OPERATION & NAVIGATION

7. ENVIRONMENTAL LAWS & REGULATIONS

8. BOATING RESTRICTIONS

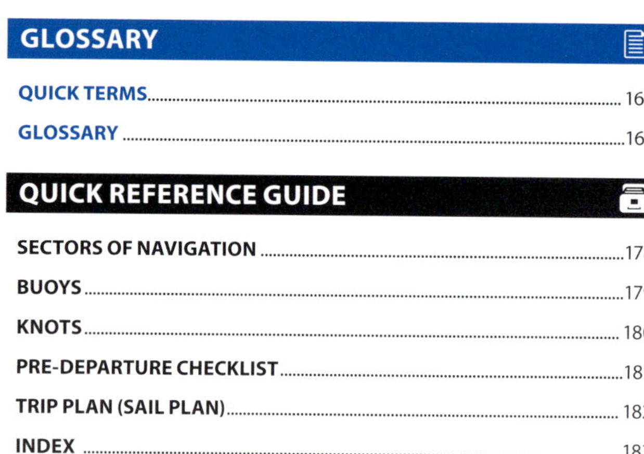

GLOSSARY

QUICK REFERENCE GUIDE

1. THE BOAT

→ Operator Competency Law

→ Boating Safety and Responsibilities

→ Boat Terminology

→ Boat Hull Designs and Uses

→ Capacity Plate and Licensing Requirements

WHAT'S THIS?
Scan these QR codes with your mobile device to access videos and exclusive content.

INTRODUCTION

Whether you're fishing, water-skiing, wakeboarding, or just going for a tour around the lake, boating is one of Canada's most pleasurable and popular outdoor activities. But operating a motorized watercraft is also a big responsibility. Your safety and that of other boaters depends on your responsible operation. This boating safety course is an important first step to making sure your time on the water stays fun-filled.

Over the years, boating safety education has made a big impact in the number of boating accidents and fatalities in Canada. According to the Lifesaving Society, between 1997 and 2007 (the last year that we have complete statistics), the number of drowning deaths related to power boating decreased from an average of 96 to 60 fatalities per year—a reduction of almost 40%! That is an amazing improvement. But we can still do better.

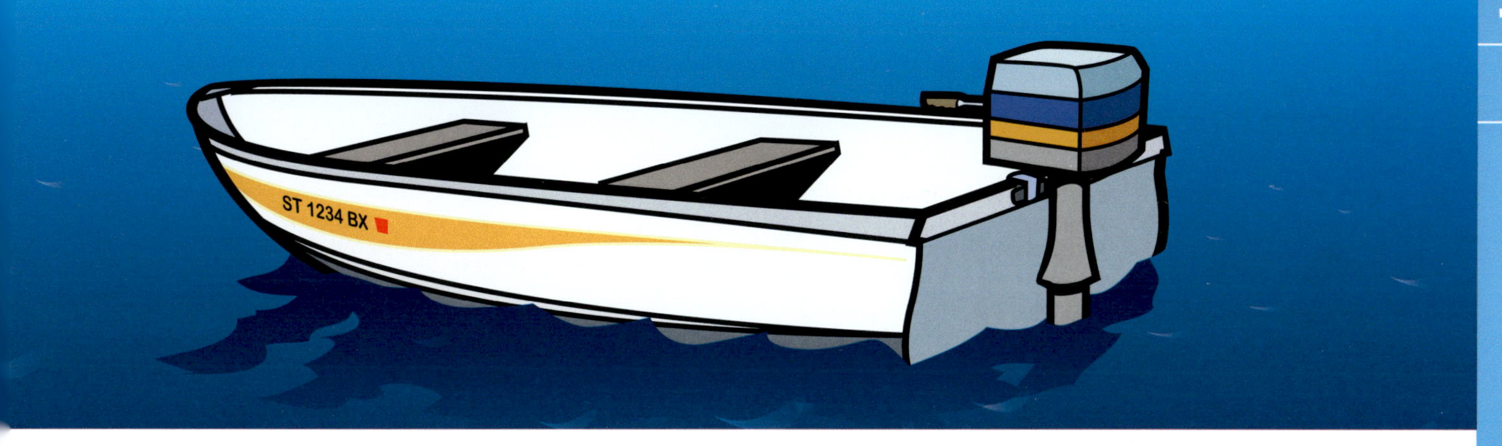

How can we do better? By treating boating safety as our number one priority at all times. That means understanding the proper way to operate a motorized watercraft, which is something you will learn in the following chapters. It also means knowing the risk factors associated with boating.

The number one cause of boating related fatalities is not wearing a personal flotation device (PFD) or lifejacket. Between the years of 2005 and 2007, 80% of drowning victims were not wearing a properly fitted PFD. So, we can vastly reduce the risks associated with boating by doing one simple thing: wearing a PFD.

Other boating safety hazards you will learn about in the course include boating under the influence, falling overboard, rough water, and capsizing in cold water. By knowing the risk factors and taking the appropriate precautions, you can stay safe, have fun, and enjoy the beauty of Canada's outdoors.

This course will provide you with an easy to follow, common-sense approach to power boating, all of the tools you need to enjoy the water safely, and to get your Pleasure Craft Operator Card. Thank you on behalf of BOATERexam.com for helping us continue to make our waters safer.

SAFETY

Operator Competency Law

In Canada, ALL operators of recreational powered watercraft must have proof of operator competency in order to operate any vessel (this includes personal watercraft and electric motors). Proof of competency must be carried onboard at all times while operating the pleasure craft. Failure to carry proof of competency can result in harsh monetary fines, which may be issued by any officer of the peace.

Proof of competency can be a Pleasure Craft Operator Card, a Boating Safety Course Completion Card, a rental boat safety checklist, proof of successful completion of a boating safety course, or a training certificate recognized by Transport Canada.

If carrying a Pleasure Craft Operator Card as proof of competency, the original card must be carried onboard. Photocopies or other copies of the card will not be accepted as proof of competency.

In the case of non-residents of Canada, they are required to have proof of operator competency if they operate their pleasure craft on Canadian waters for more than 44 consecutive days, or if they are operating a pleasure craft that is registered or licensed in Canada. An operator card that meets requirements in the non-resident's home state or country will be recognized as valid proof of competency in Canada.

NOTE: *For more information on additional proofs of competency that are recognized by Transport Canada, please visit www.boatingsafety.gc.ca, or call the Boating Safety Infoline at 1-800-267-6687.*

Small-vessel safety equipment and safety precaution requirements for boaters include a *careless operation of a vessel* offence, which requires boaters to travel safely and avoid putting themselves and others at risk.

Age/Horsepower Restrictions

AGE	HORSEPOWER RESTRICTIONS
Under 12 years of age with no direct supervision	May only operate a boat with a motor up to 10 hp, unless accompanied and directly supervised by someone 16 years of age or older.
Ages 12 to under 16 with no direct supervision	May only operate a boat with a motor up to 40 hp, unless accompanied and directly supervised by someone 16 years of age or older.
Under 16 years of age, regardless of supervision	May not operate a PWC. (i.e., Sea-Doo®, Jet Ski®)
16 years of age or older	No horsepower restrictions.

Know Before You Go

Avoid danger on the water by taking a few minutes before you leave to check the following:

- Weather forecast.
- Local hazards.
- Maps and charts.
- Your onboard PFDs.
- First-aid kit, tool kit, tools and spare parts onboard.
- Sufficient fuel.
- Safety equipment in working order.
- Ensure that someone knows where you are going and when to expect you back.

Wear Your Lifejacket or Personal Flotation Device

The major cause of fatalities involving small boats is drowning from falls overboard, which is why it is important for boaters to wear their lifejacket or Personal Flotation Device (PFD). In fact, research indicates that only 15% of all drowning victims were wearing a lifejacket or PFD at the time of death. However, fewer than half of all who wear a PFD wear it properly. All boaters should wear PFDs when in and around water, not just when operating or riding in a vessel.

Wear the Right Gear

When boating, wear good-quality sunglasses and appropriate clothing, including a PFD or lifejacket.

Boat Sober!

Don't drink and drive—that applies just as much to operating a boat as it does to operating a motor vehicle. Although the numbers of reported impaired boat operators are decreasing, alcohol use is still a major factor in more than 40% of all preventable water-related fatalities, and over half of all power boating accidents.

Drive Your Powerboat or Personal Watercraft Responsibly

Capsizing, collisions and falls overboard are all leading causes of boating-related fatalities. Look before you act, sit low in the boat, drive at moderate speed, and be aware of changing weather conditions as well as the time of day. Never overload your boat and always respect the Compliance Notice (*see page 13*) for small boats.

Bring Your Marine Global Positioning System (GPS) or Nautical Charts (Marine Charts)

Increasing in popularity over the past few years, GPS devices can be extremely helpful while on the water; however a GPS is a mechanical device and can fail. Having the appropriate nautical charts (also known as marine charts) onboard are also a great asset, and should be available in case the GPS does not work properly. This is especially important when boating on unfamiliar waterways.

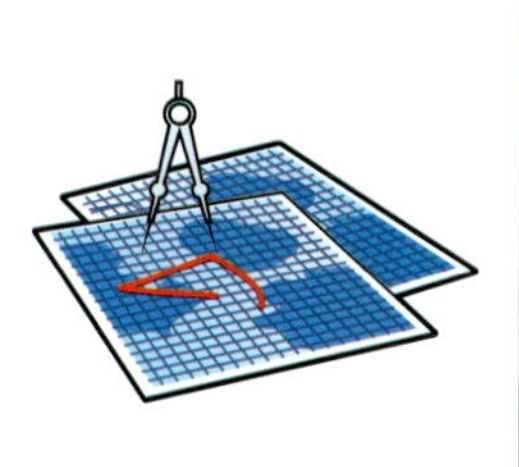

BOAT TERMINOLOGY

Specific terms are used to describe the various parts of a boat. Each end and side of the boat, its length and width, and its accessories have specific terms. Every boater should be familiar with the following terms before operating a boat.

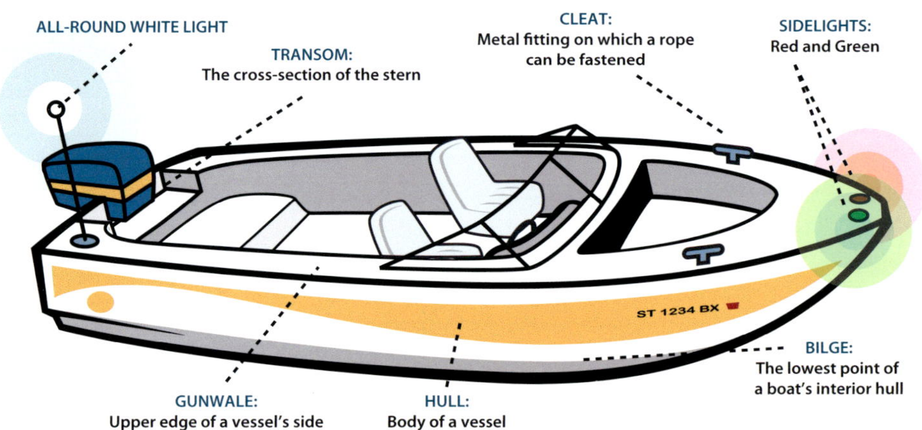

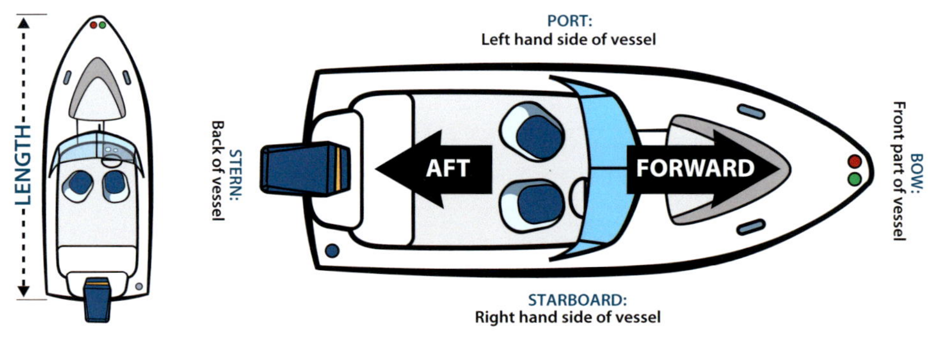

Additional Terminology

Here are some additional terms that boaters should be familiar with before operating a boat:

Aft
Located near or at the stern of the boat.

Beam
The width of a boat at the widest point.

Bilge
The lowest point of a boat's interior hull.

Draft
The vertical distance from the waterline to the lowest point of the keel; the minimum depth of water in which a vessel will float.

Forward
Located near, or at the bow of the boat.

Freeboard
The vertical distance from the waterline to the gunwale.

Keel
The main structural member of a boat comprising its backbone plus the lateral area beneath the hull, helping to provide stability and reduce the sideways drift of a boat.

Waterline
The intersection of a boat's hull and the water's surface.

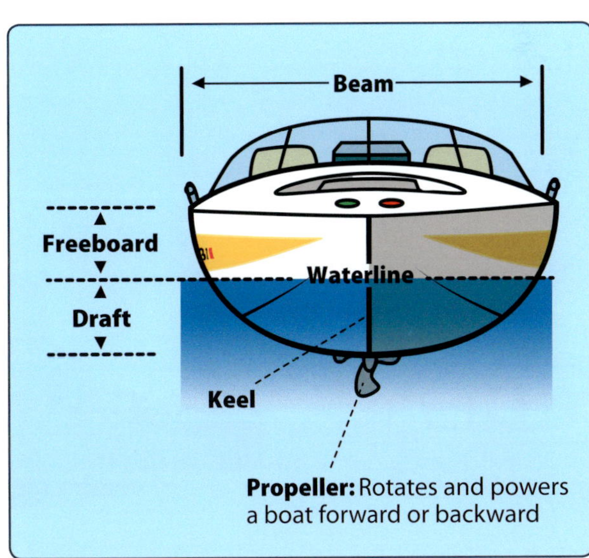

BOAT HULL DESIGNS AND USES

Boat bottoms or hulls are available in a variety of shapes and sizes. Each hull type is designed either to displace or plane through the water. Sailing vessels and large cruise ships use displacement hulls because the combination of their size and power will not allow them to plane. On the other hand, smaller powerboats are typically built with planing hulls that are designed to rise up and ride on top of the water at higher speeds than displacement hull boats.

Hull Types

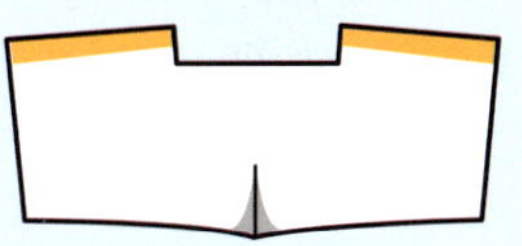

Flat-Bottom

Great for fishing, and are generally designed for slow speeds and calm water.

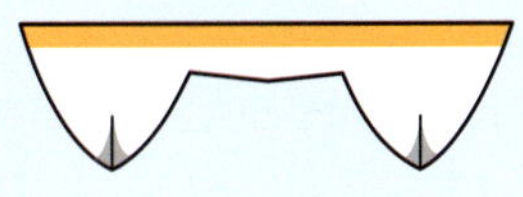

Multi-Hull

The most stable of the hull types, these boats require plenty of room to steer and turn.

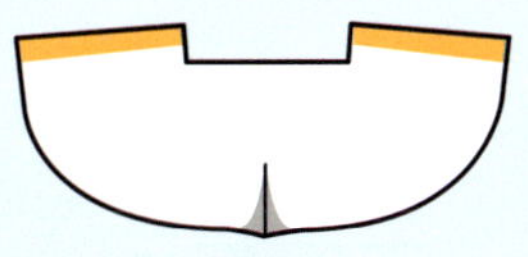

Round-Bottom

While these boats, such as canoes, move smoothly through the water with little effort, boaters must be cautious when loading, entering and exiting those with this type of hull because they roll very easily.

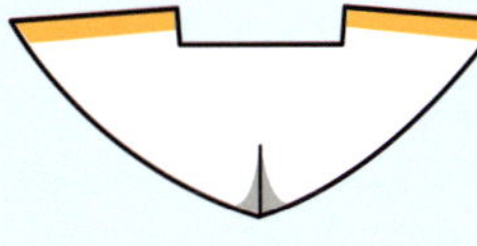

Deep-V Hull

This is the most common hull type for powerboats, which moves through rough water at higher speeds and give a smoother ride than flat-bottom or round-bottom boats. It also requires a larger engine than other boats.

ENGINE TYPES

Outboard

Mounted on the transom of the boat, an outboard can be controlled by a hand tiller or a steering wheel, which moves the entire engine when steering is adjusted. In the past, outboards were typically two-stroke engines, but manufacturers have since switched to four-stroke engines. Two-stroke engines require oil to be mixed with gasoline to lubricate the engine and four-stroke engines require the oil and gasoline to be separate. Four-stroke engines, in addition to running more quietly and smoothly, are more environmentally friendly because their exhaust is virtually smokeless compared to two-strokes.

Inboard

These are typically four-stroke automotive engines that are modified for use on the water. An inboard engine is mounted inside the hull of the boat and powers the driveshaft through the boat bottom, which is connected to a propeller. Steering is controlled by a rudder, positioned either directly behind or to the side of the propeller.

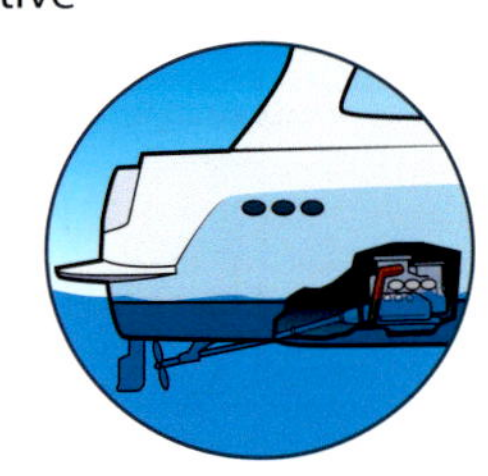

Sterndrives

These are sometimes called inboard/outboards (I/O) because they have features found on both inboard and outboard engines. Similar to inboards, a sterndrive uses a four-stroke automotive engine that is modified for use on the water. It is mounted inside the boat through the transom, and powers the drive train, which is connected to the propeller. Similar to outboards, the sterndrive moves when the steering wheel is adjusted.

Compliance Notice for an outboard powered vessel of not more than 6 metres

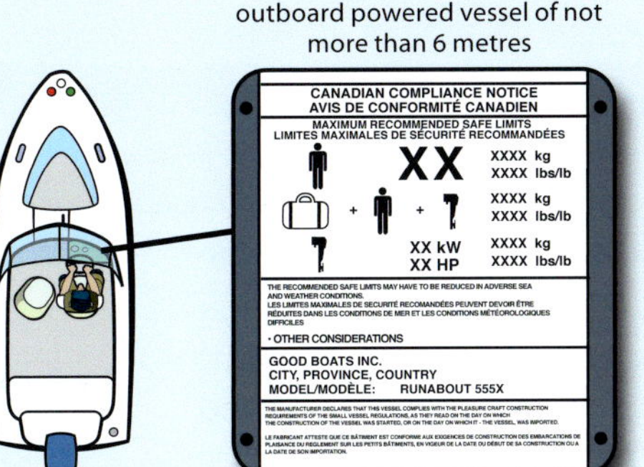

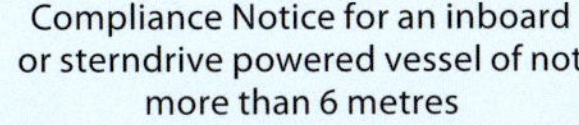
Compliance Notice for an inboard or sterndrive powered vessel of not more than 6 metres

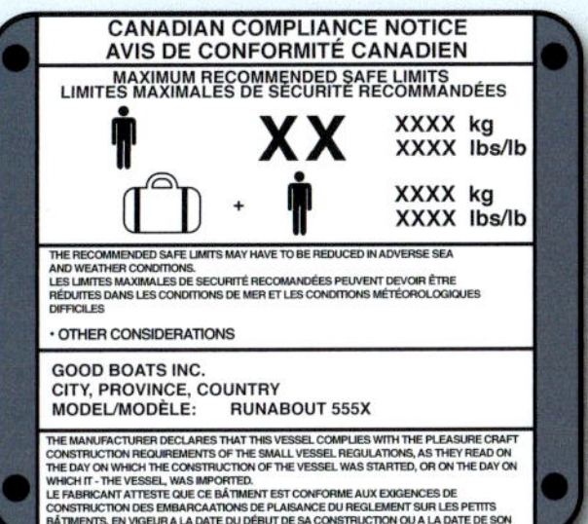

Compliance Notice for Pleasure Craft of more than 6 metres

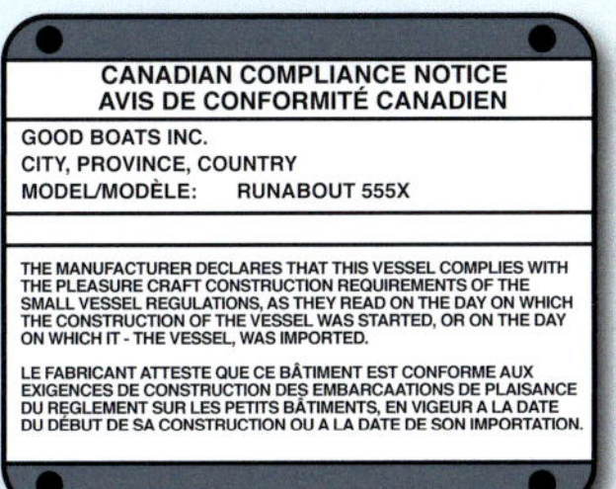

CONFORMITY PLATES AND REQUIREMENTS RELATIVE TO PERMITS

Compliance Notice

All pleasure craft under 24 m in length that are motorized or designed to be motorized, must have a compliance notice. For vessels less than 6 m in length, the compliance notice indicates the maximum gross load to be carried, including but not limited to the total weight of all persons, fuel, and any equipment onboard.

The compliance notice for vessels of 6 m or less should indicate the *maximum recommended safe limits for motor power* for the hull. This limit must never be surpassed. This calculation is based on the gross load capacity of the vessel powered by an outboard motor only.

As owner or operator of a vessel, you must be aware of the gross load capacity that the hull can safely transport, during fair weather. Remember that a loaded boat is more prone to swamping, and that chances of swamping or capsizing can be decreased by reducing your load in poor weather or rough water.

HULL IDENTIFICATION NUMBER

Hull Identification Number

According to the Canada Shipping Act 2001, all pleasure craft (with OR without a motor) manufactured in, or imported into Canada after August 1, 1981, must be permanently marked with a Hull Identification Number (HIN) on the starboard side of the stern. This 12-character serial number is often used to help identify lost or stolen vessels. If you are purchasing a vessel, it is important to make sure it has a HIN. It is illegal to alter or otherwise tamper with a Hull Identification Number.

Pleasure Craft Licences

A Pleasure Craft Licence refers to the set of identification numbers to be displayed on both sides of your boat's bow. All pleasure craft principally maintained or operated in Canada propelled by motors of 10 horsepower (7.5 kW) or greater must be licensed, unless they have been registered. This includes personal watercraft. Alternatively to licensing your boat, you can register it with Transport Canada.

It is the responsibility of the person owning or operating the pleasure craft to ensure that the licence is onboard and available upon request by an enforcement officer. There are no fees to obtain a Pleasure Craft Licence.

Pleasure Craft Licence is Not a Registration

Vessel registration is the title of ownership of a boat or vessel, which includes the official vessel name and the name of the owner(s). Although not required for pleasure craft, they can be registered on a voluntary basis at the owner's discretion. Registration is valid for three years, and fees vary depending on the type of vessel and type of registration. For more information, please consult with Transport Canada's Vessel Registry at *www.tc.gc.ca*.

Change in Name or Address

Pleasure Craft Licences are valid for a period of 10 years. If the owner's name or address changes, the licence must be updated with the Pleasure Craft Licensing Centre. The pleasure craft may be operated without an accurate name and/or date on the licence for up to 90 days, as long as documents are carried onboard that confirm the change and the date of change. Applications for licence updates are available from the Pleasure Craft Licensing Centre online at *www.boatingsafety.gc.ca* or for pickup in person through your local Service Canada Centre.

Transferring your Licence

If the ownership of a licenced pleasure craft is transferred, the former owner must sign the transfer form that is printed on the reverse side of the licence and deliver it to the new owner. The new owner will then be required to submit an application form along with the required documentation by mail to the Pleasure Craft Licensing Centre to transfer the Pleasure Craft Licence. The pleasure craft can be operated for a maximum of 90 days without a licence, as long as the new owner has applied for a licence, and carries proof of name and address onboard. For more information on the sale or transfer of a Pleasure Craft Licence, visit the Office of Boating Safety or call the Boating Safety InfoLine at 1-800-267-6687.

Display your Licence Number

All licensed vessels must display the licence number in block letters that are at least 7.5 centimeters (3″) in height.

The licence number must also:

- Be displayed, above the waterline, on both sides of the vessel's bow.
- Be in contrast with the colour of the background.

> **NOTE:** *For more information on pleasure craft licences, please consult the* Small Vessel Regulations *under the* Canada Shipping Act.
> *www.tc.gc.ca/eng/acts-regulations/acts-2001c26.htm*

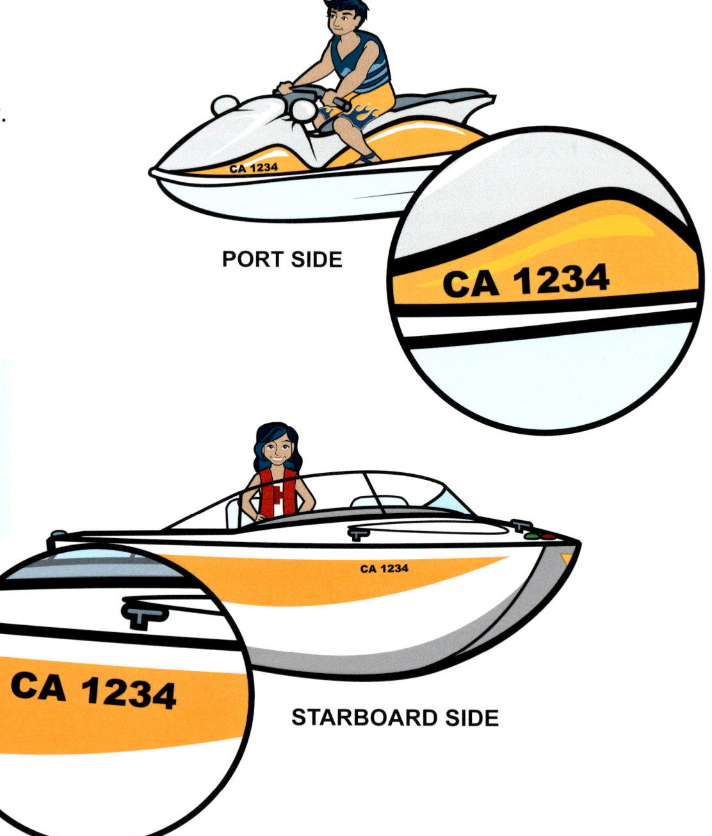

The Boat

Let's review the important parts of this chapter:

- In Canada, ALL operators of recreational powered watercraft must have proof of operator competency in order to operate a motorized vessel (this includes personal watercraft and boats fitted with electric or gasoline motors).
- The major cause of fatalities involving small boats is drowning from falls overboard, which is why it is important for boaters to wear their life jacket or Personal Flotation Device (PFD).
- Specific terms are used to describe the various parts of a boat. Each end and side of the boat, its length and width, and its accessories have specific terms that all boaters should be familiar with.
- Boat bottoms or hulls are available in a variety of shapes and sizes. Each hull type is designed either to displace or plane through the water.
- There are three main engine types for recreational watercraft—Outboard, Inboard, and Sterndrives.
- All powered pleasure craft in Canada must have a Compliance Notice, and a Capacity Plate or Conformity Plate.
- All licensed vessels must display the licence number in block letters that are at least 7.5 cm in height and the colour must be in contrast with the colour of the background of the boat.

1. Persons under the age of 12 are permitted to operate a power-driven vessel above 10 hp only if which of the following conditions are met?

A. They are directly supervised by someone over 16 years of age

B. They are wearing an approved lifejacket

C. They are operating within 200 m of a shoreline

D. They are operating a boat owned by a family member

2. Hull Identification Numbers (HINs) are used to properly identify a vessel and are marked on which of the following locations?

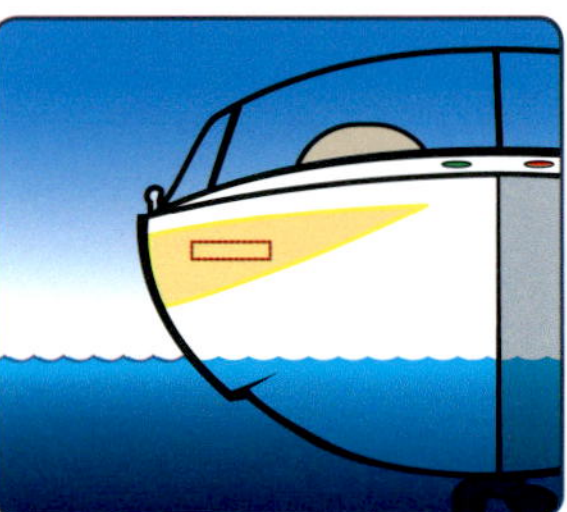

A. Starboard side of the bow

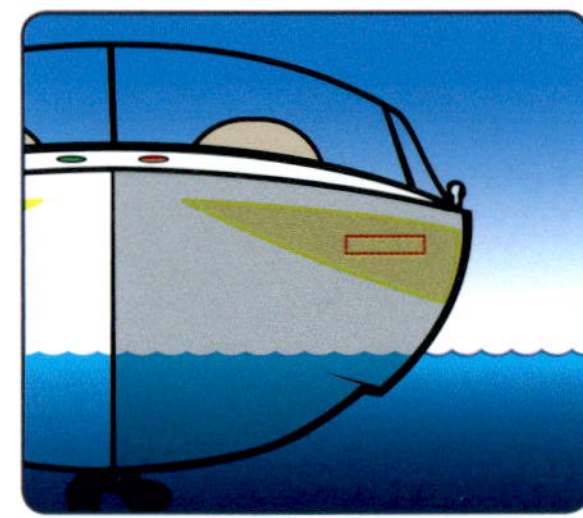

B. Port side of the bow

C. Port side of the stern

D. Starboard side of the stern

3. Which of the following can result in harsh monetary fines?

A. Operating a power-driven vessel after sunset

B. Operating a PWC (personal watercraft) within 200 m of a shoreline

C. Operating a power-driven vessel without proof of operator competency

D. Pulling a water skier with a power-driven vessel

4. Research indicates that ONLY 15% of drowning victims were doing which of the following at the time of their death?

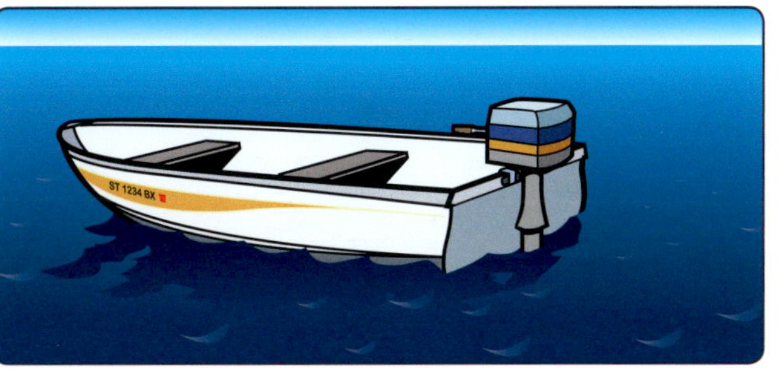

A. Wearing a Personal Flotation Device

B. Wearing sunglasses

C. Attempting to swim to shore

D. Attempting to re-board a boat

Quiz Answers	1.a • 2.d • 3.c • 4.a

2. BOATING EQUIPMENT

- → Lifejackets and Personal Flotation Devices
- → Boating Equipment
- → Fire Extinguishers
- → Distress Signalling
- → Navigation Lights
- → Navigational Aids

PROPER CARE AND USE OF PERSONAL FLOTATION DEVICES

About Personal Flotation Devices

Personal Flotation Devices (PFDs) and lifejackets can save lives and should be worn while boating whenever a vessel is in operation. If not worn, they must be readily accessible. Therefore, Transport Canada requires that there be at least one approved PFD or lifejacket for each person onboard a vessel. When choosing a PFD, ensure that it can support the size and weight of the wearer.

It is the responsibility of the boat operator to ensure there are properly fitted PFDs onboard for all passengers. If not worn, inform all passengers of the location of the PFDs, and ensure passengers know how to put on their PFD properly. Before heading out on the water, it's a good idea for all passengers to test their PFD (*see page 23*). Always follow manufacturer's instructions when using a PFD.

In Canada, flotation devices are categorized into three different types:

Lifejackets

Personal Flotation Devices (PFDs)

Inflatable lifejackets/PFDs

For a Personal Flotation Device to be approved in Canada, it must have a label stating that it has been approved by Transport Canada, the Canadian Coast Guard, Fisheries and Oceans Canada, or any combination of these three organizations.

Approved Lifejackets

Lifejackets and Personal Flotation Devices can both bear Canadian approval; however in order for a lifejacket to be approved, it must be red, orange or yellow in colour, and designed to turn the wearer face-up when in the water. There are three basic types of lifejackets:

- The SOLAS (Safety of Life At Sea) lifejacket offers the greatest amount of buoyancy and will turn the wearer face-up very quickly.
- The standard type lifejacket has a standard level of buoyancy and will be slightly slower at turning the wearer face-up when in the water. When laid out flat, they resemble a keyhole shape.
- The small vessel lifejacket is designed for calm, inland waters. It will turn the wearer face-up; however it has a slower performance since it does not offer as much buoyancy as other lifejacket types.

Testing a Personal Flotation Device

Be sure you know the following technique to test Personal Flotation Devices and/or lifejackets:

1. While wearing the Personal Flotation Device and/or lifejacket…
2. in chest-deep water…
3. the person shall bend the knees…
4. then float on the back, and…
5. ensure that the PFD or lifejacket keeps their chin above water so that it's easy for them to breathe.

PFD Sizing

To ensure that the PFD fits properly, have the wearer put it on and adjust straps as necessary to make it fit snugly. A properly fitted PFD will not ride higher than the wearer's ears or mouth.

When to Replace a PFD

Make sure your PFDs are in good shape before you go boating. Regularly check for rips and tears. In particular, check straps and hardware before you leave the dock. PFDs with rips, tears or other damage will NOT receive Canadian approval and you may be fined.

APPROVED

NOT APPROVED

Cleaning a Lifejacket or PFD

When cleaning a PFD, it is important to:

- Use mild soap, never a detergent.
- Never dry your PFD close to a direct heat source, nor dry-clean it.
- Air dry your PFD in a well-ventilated space that's not exposed to direct sunlight.
- Never use your PFD as a cushion for kneeling, sitting or as a fender.

Regularly check PFDs for buoyancy: while wearing your PFD, wade into waist-height water, bend your knees, lean backwards and ensure that you are floating sufficiently.

Inflatable PFDs

Inflatable Personal Flotation Devices are available in two styles:

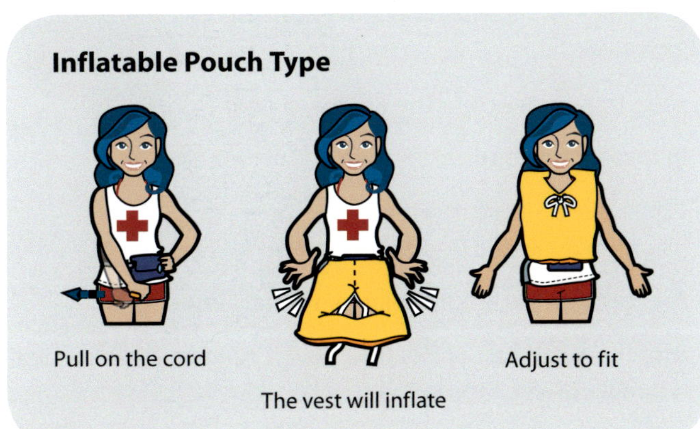

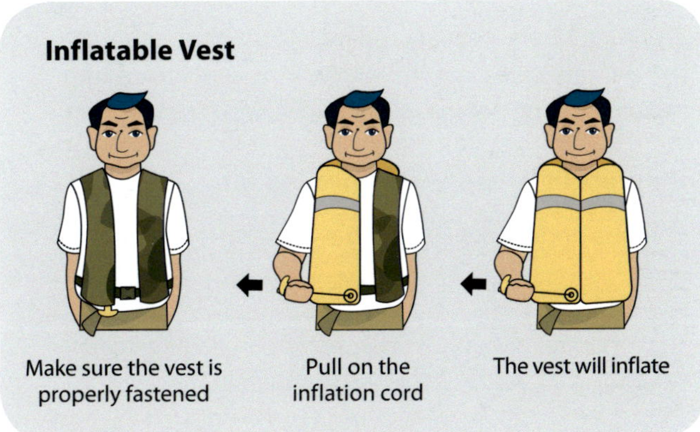

Pouch Types

These are worn around the waist and can be inflated orally or manually by pulling a toggle (chord) to activate a CO_2 inflation system.

Vest Types

These are worn similar to a PFD and are inflated either orally, manually using a chord (activating the CO_2 inflation system), or automatically (upon detection of water the CO_2 system inflates the vest).

Inflatable type PFDs are considered approved if they are:

- Worn in any open boat.
- Worn by a person in any boat that is not open while the person is on deck, in the cockpit, or if it is readily available to the person when the person is below deck.

Inflatable PFDs are NOT approved for:

- Persons under 16 years of age.
- Persons weighing less than 36.3 kg (80 lbs).
- High-impact activities, such as personal watercraft operation or white-water paddling activities.
- PFDs fitted with an automatic inflator may not be used by a person on a sailboard.

An inflatable lifejacket is not inherently buoyant, and will not float until it is inflated. For this reason, it is advisable they only be used by strong swimmers.

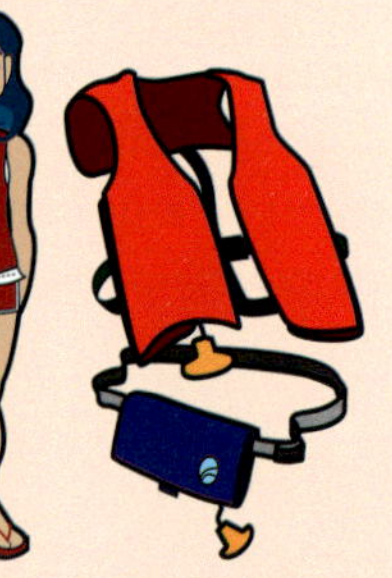

BOAT SAFETY EQUIPMENT

Buoyant Heaving Lines

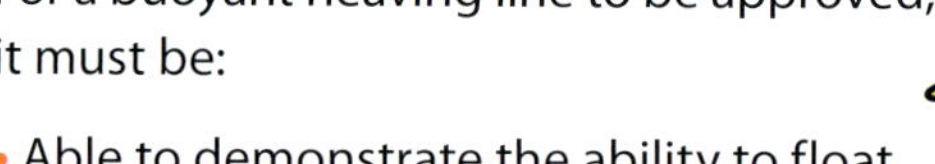

For a buoyant heaving line to be approved, it must be:

- Able to demonstrate the ability to float.
- In good condition.
- Consist of a single, full length of rope (i.e., shorter ropes tied together are not approved).
- An appropriate length relative to the vessel.
- Attached to a ball or floating object to increase accuracy when thrown to someone overboard.
- Used only as safety equipment.
- Stowed in a place where it can be easily accessed in an emergency.

A buoyant heaving line can be difficult to throw accurately. Practice throwing the line in a controlled setting before you get out on the water, so that you are able to throw it accurately in an emergency situation.

Lifebuoys

Lifebuoys are required for all vessels over 9 m in length. They must also be approved by Transport Canada and have an approval stamp or label.

There are two types of lifebuoys:

- The small vessel lifebuoy that is 610 mm in diameter.
- The SOLAS lifebuoy that is 762 mm in diameter.

> **NOTE**: *Buoys less than 610 mm (24") in diameter are not considered approved by Transport Canada.*

To be approved a lifebuoy must be attached to a buoyant heaving line that is secure and in good condition. Any smaller lifebuoys as well as horseshoe-style devices are not approved for boating use. Lifebuoys that have tears, perforations or rot are not approved.

Re-boarding Devices

Vessels that have more than 0.5 m of freeboard are required to have some sort of re-boarding device onboard to allow a person who is in the water to get back into the boat. This requirement can be met with either a transom ladder or a swim platform ladder. Re-boarding devices must be separate from the propulsion unit.

Manual Propelling Device

A manual propelling device can mean a set of oars, a paddle or any other apparatus that can be used by a person to propel a vessel by hand.

It is important to ensure that the manual propelling device is strong enough for its intended use. For example, a 1 m plastic oar is not of sufficient strength to propel a 12 m fishing boat.

Anchors

All anchors are attached to a cable, which is comprised of a rope and chain. Also referred to as a "*rode*". The length of rode to have out depends on the water depth in which you plan to set anchor. Your rode length should be 5 to 10 times the depth of the water in which you are anchoring. Anchors can be of assistance in emergency situations—especially in case of engine failure in rough waters or currents—and to prevent the boat from drifting. Make sure the anchor is always accessible and the rode is free of entanglements.

There are a number of anchor types to choose from. The most common recreational anchors are listed below. Choose the anchor type that meets your requirements.

Danforth
Pivoting flukes bury the anchor. Best for soft mud and seagrass.

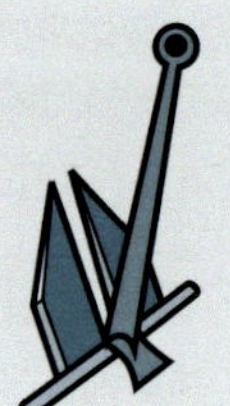

Mushroom
For canoes and inflatables. Best for flat bottoms.

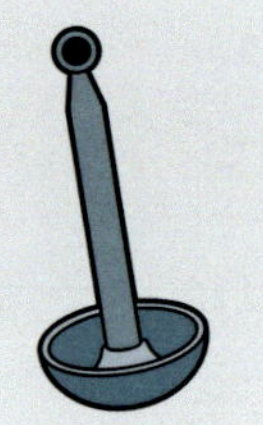

Plow
Lands sideways and buries when pulled. Best for rocky bottoms, weeds, and seagrass.

Tips for Anchoring

- Before you drop the anchor, ensure it has a locking device so that you don't lose your anchor while in the water.
- Remember: the wind or tide will move your boat around the anchor; you should allow a 360-degree area for movement.
- Pick a spot upwind from where you wish to end up (once you set anchor, you will drift downwind).
- Calculate the amount of cable (rode) needed to set anchor (rode = 5-10 x water depth).
- Ready the rode in a fashion that will allow the anchor to release smoothly to the bottom; ensure that no feet or equipment are entangled in the rope.
- Slowly lower the anchor from the bow (*never from the stern*).
- When the anchor has hit bottom - and sufficient rode is given out - give a solid pull to set the anchor.
- Secure the rode to a bow cleat (*never tie to the stern: the additional weight could bring on water*).

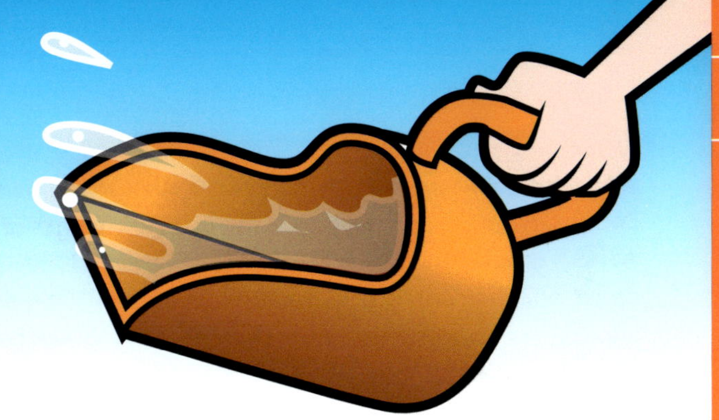

Bailers and Manual Water Pumps

A bailer refers to a container that is capable of removing water from a small vessel. A bailer must be made of plastic or metal, have an opening of at least 65 cm^2 and be capable of holding at least 750 mL of water. Some boats may carry a manual water pump in place of a bailer. If this is the case for your boat, the pump along with its hose must be long enough to reach from the bilge to the boat's side and be capable of discharging water over the side of the boat.

> **NOTE:** *Larger vessels are usually equipped with a mechanical bilge that's very fast and effective at removing water from the bilge.*

Fire Buckets

The *Canadian Small Vessel Regulations* require vessels more than 9 m in length to carry fire bucket(s) onboard in case of a fire emergency. These buckets must have a round bottom with a hole in the center, be red in colour, and must have a capacity of 10 L or more in order to be approved. They should have a line attached which is long enough to reach the water from the gunwale.

Fire Extinguishers

Fire extinguishers are classified according to the type and size of fire they can handle. See chapter 3 (*page 60*) for fire extinguisher requirements for your vessel.

Axe

The axe is required as safety equipment on recreational boats 12 m or longer. It can be used in emergency situations to cut tow lines or other ropes. The axe must be in a readily accessible location on the boat, and protected from the elements.

FIRE TYPES AND FIRE EXTINGUISHERS

There are three types of fires:

CLASS A

Those involving combustible solids, such as wood.

CLASS B

Those involving flammable liquids, such as gasoline and oil.

CLASS C

Those involving electrical fires.

Wood or paper fires (Class A) can be handled and extinguished with water. However, water should never be applied to electrical (Class C) or flammable liquid (Class B) fires, as the water will only spread flammable liquid fires and will conduct electricity. Most fire extinguishers are suitable for putting out Class B and C fires. Marine fire extinguishers must be capable of extinguishing Class B AND Class C fires (Class BC fire extinguisher).

The size of fire that a fire extinguisher can handle is indicated by the number before the letters. The greater the number, the bigger the fire it can handle. For instance, a 10BC extinguisher is capable of putting out a larger fire than a 5BC extinguisher. Be sure you know what type of fire extinguisher is required onboard your boat (*see chapter 3*) and always check to make sure it is fully charged.

Fire extinguishers must be certified and labelled by the U.S. Coast Guard (for marine use), Underwriters Laboratories of Canada (ULC) or the Underwriters Laboratories, Inc. (UL).

NOTE: *Please refer to the manufacturer's instructions for the proper Fire Extinguisher Safety.*

Fire Extinguisher Safety

As a life-saving tool, your fire extinguisher should be kept in proper functioning order.

Take the following steps to help ensure that your fire extinguisher is safe and ready for use:

- Avoid placing your fire extinguisher in areas of high temperature.
- Replace any old or used fire extinguisher immediately (even if used only once).
- Have rechargeable fire extinguishers refilled by a qualified professional.
- Read and follow all of the manufacturer's instructions.
- Shake it! To prevent clumping of the chemicals inside, shake the fire extinguisher upside-down; every month!
- Inspect it for damage (i.e, broken seals, pins, other damage, etc.) on a regular basis.

NOTE: *The type of fire extinguisher required on a boat depends on the length of the boat and type of appliances onboard; be sure you know what type of fire extinguisher is required onboard your boat (see chapter 3 for details).*

**ALWAYS keep your fire extinguisher in a convenient and easily accessible location!*

DISTRESS EQUIPMENT AND DISTRESS SIGNALLING

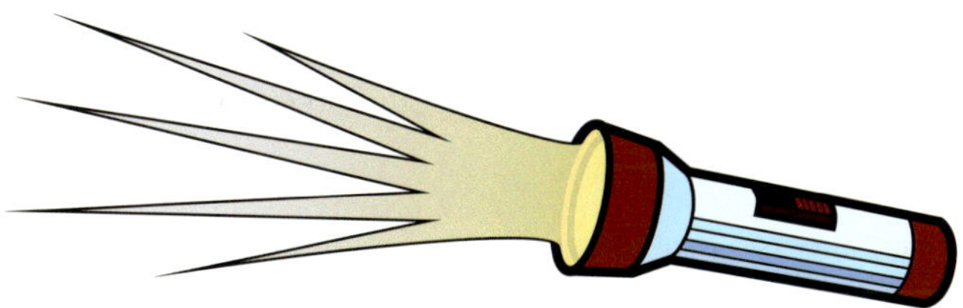

Watertight Flashlights

Always be prepared for unforeseen situations when boating. Since you cannot predict when navigation lights will burn out or when day trips might last beyond nightfall, every vessel must have a flashlight onboard. Before every trip, always ensure your flashlight is functioning properly. It's always wise to bring extra batteries with you as well. A flashlight can be a very useful tool if you need to signal for help in an emergency situation.

NOTE: *The watertight flashlight can be used as navigation lights for unpowered vessels as well as sailboats that are under 7 m in length.*

Standard Marine Distress Signals

If you see a distress signal, you are required by law to determine whether you can assist those in distress without endangering your own life or safety of your vessel. Where possible, you must also contact the nearest Rescue Coordination Centre to inform them of the type and location of the distress signal you have seen.

Never send a false distress signal. Not only is it against the law to make a false distress signal, but false alarms commit search and rescue personnel, making them potentially unavailable or farther away from real emergencies.

Distress Signals (use anytime)

Knowing the following distress signals will help you call for help in an emergency and recognize those in trouble.

Marine Radio Distress Call

Use 2182 kHz (MF) or channel 16, 156.8 MHz (VHF) DSC alert, channel 70 (only for DSC type radios and where the service is offered).

Calling Procedures

In a distress situation, use the marine radio to communicate the following:

- *Mayday, Mayday, Mayday*—Immediate danger to persons or ship.
- *Pan-Pan, Pan-Pan, Pan-Pan*—Urgent message concerning safety of a person or ship.

In addition, you must communicate in your message:

- The name of your vessel and call sign.
- The position of your vessel.
- A description of the nature of the emergency.

Sound Signals

Sound signals are sent by emitting a continuous sound with any sound signalling apparatus. This includes firing a gun or other explosive signal at one-minute intervals.

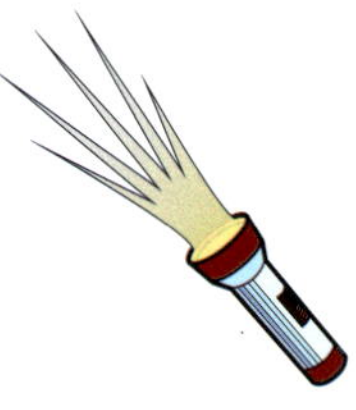

Flashlight

A flashlight can be used to send a distress signal by flashing an S.O.S. signal, which consists of three short bursts, three long bursts, followed again by three short bursts (i.e., short-short-short, long-long-long, short-short-short).

Emergency Position Indicating Radio Beacon (EPIRB)

You can also send a distress signal by activating the alarm signal on a Emergency Position Indicating Radio Beacon, located in your boat.

Distress Signals (Daytime Use)

In addition to distress signals that can be used at any time, there are several that can be used in daylight conditions.

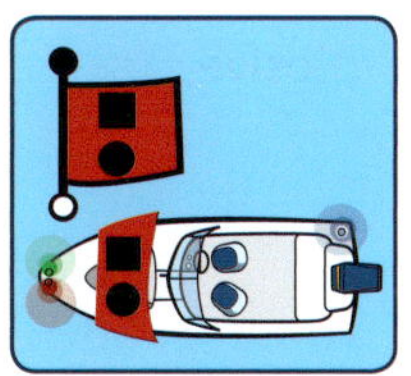

Distress Cloth

To attract attention, spread a distress cloth on cabin or deck top of the boat, or fly it from the mast.

Code Flags

Code flags can be raised to indicate distress. These flags consist of:

- Ball over or under square.
- N over C.

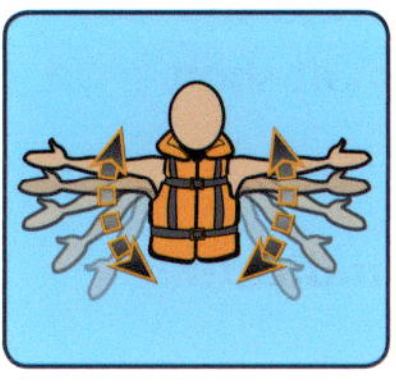

Arm Signal

Raising and lowering outstretched arms repeatedly is also a commonly understood distress signal.

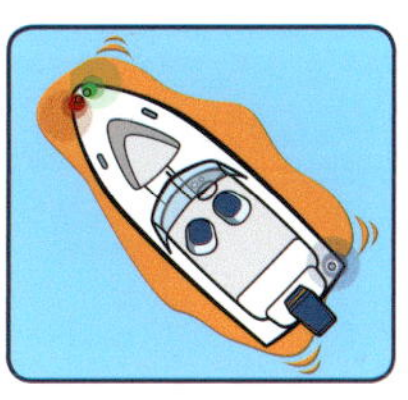

Dye Marker

In a distress situation, you can also attract attention by releasing orange dye into the water.

Flares

Pyrotechnic distress signals (flares) must be Transport Canada approved, in serviceable condition and not expired.

The number of flares required depends on the length of the vessel and its area of operation. See chapter 3 for the number of flares required onboard your boat. Always read and follow all the manufacturer's instructions before using flares.

> * **NOTE:** *Flares should be stored in a cool, dry location and must be readily accessible in case of an emergency.*

Your local retailer will be able to instruct you on how to dispose of outdated flares.

Take care to prevent puncturing or otherwise damaging their coverings. Store your flares vertically in a watertight container, painted red or orange and prominently marked *DISTRESS SIGNALS*.

If young children are frequently aboard your boat, careful selection and proper stowage of visual distress signals is also important.

> * **NOTE:** *Transport Canada approved pyrotechnic devices carry a manufactured date and are only valid for four years from that date.*

Four types of flares are approved for use by Transport Canada:

- Rocket parachute flares (type A).
- Multi-star flares (type B).
- Hand flares (type C).
- Buoyant or Hand Smoke Signals (type D).

NAVIGATION EQUIPMENT

Navigation Lights

Boat operators are required to ensure their vessel is equipped with the proper navigation lights when away from the dock between sunset and sunrise, and during periods of reduced visibility such as fog or rain. Lights must be plainly visible at different distances, depending on the length of the vessel (*refer to Rule 22 in the Collision Regulations for more details*). To navigate safely during hours of darkness or periods of restricted visibility, vessel operators need to be able to interpret the various navigation light combinations. Always test your vessel's lights before heading out on the water, and replace any burnt-out bulbs before you leave.

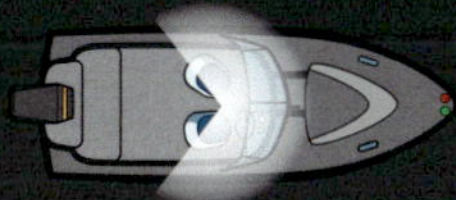

Masthead Light

A white light placed over the vessel's front and rear centreline, showing an unbroken light over an arc of the horizon of 225 degrees toward the front of the vessel.

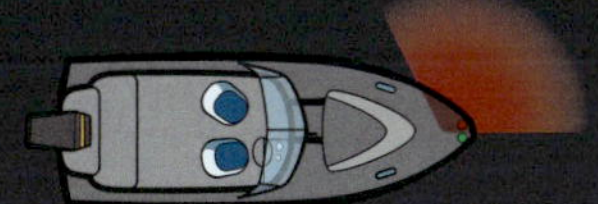

Port Sidelight

A red light on the port side showing an unbroken light over an arc of the horizon of 112.5 degrees.

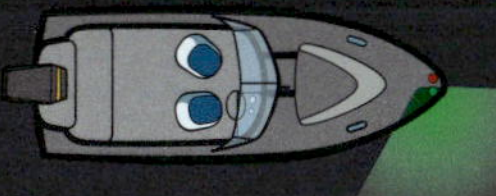

Starboard Sidelight

A green light on the starboard side showing an unbroken light over an arc of the horizon of 112.5 degrees.

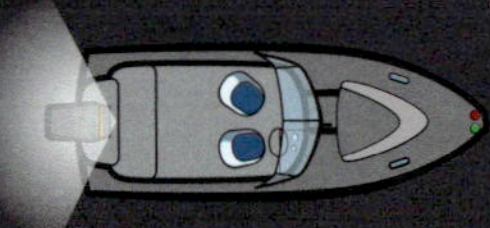

Sternlight

A white light placed as nearly as practicable at the stern, showing an unbroken light over an arc of the horizon of 135 degrees, toward the rear of the vessel.

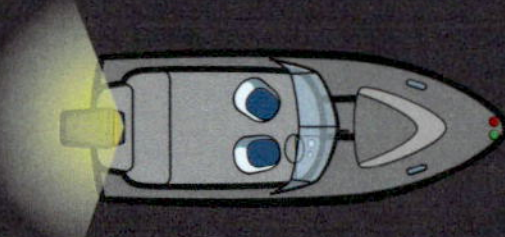

Towing Light

A yellow light having the same characteristics as a sternlight.

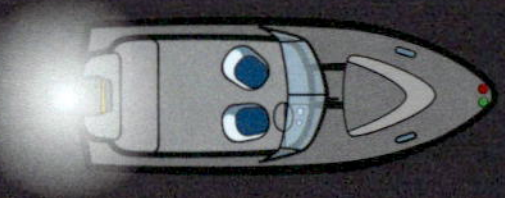

All-Round Light

A light showing an unbroken light over an arc of the horizon of 360 degrees.

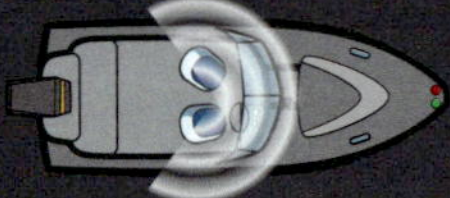

Flashing Light

A light flashing at regular intervals at a frequency of 120 flashes or more per minute.

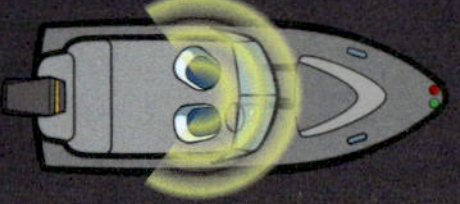

Special Flashing Light

A yellow light flashing at regular intervals at a frequency of 50 to 70 flashes per minute, placed as far forward (and near as practicable) on the fore and aft centreline of a vessel and showing an unbroken light over an arc of the horizon of not less than 180 degrees, nor more than 225 degrees (toward the front of the vessel.)

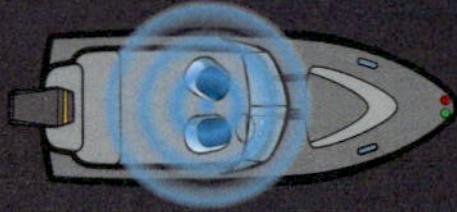

Blue Flashing Light

A blue all-round light flashing at regular intervals at a frequency of 50 to 70 flashes per minute.

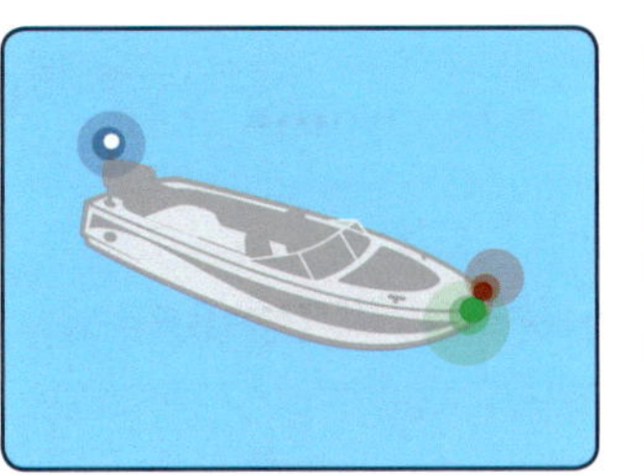

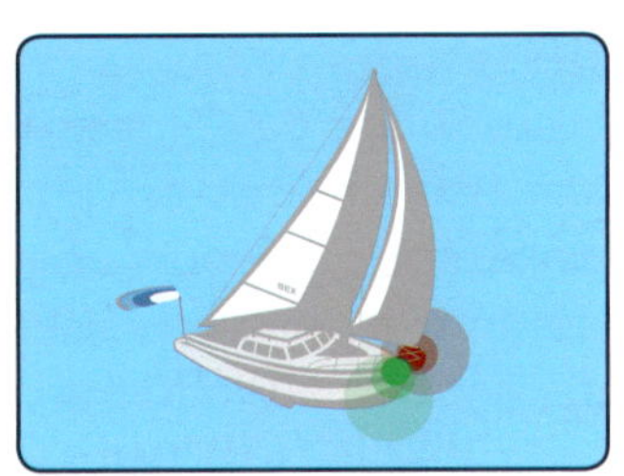

Power-Driven Vessels

Any motor-driven vessel that is operating under periods of darkness or reduced visibility must display the following lights:

- **Sidelights** - Featuring a red light on the port side (112.5 degrees), plus a green light on the starboard side (112.5 degrees); and
- **An All-Round Light** - Either an all-round white light at (or close to) the stern (360 degrees) or, if more than 12 meters in length, a white masthead light (225 degrees forward) accompanied by a sternlight (135 degrees aft), which, when combined, results in 360 degrees of white light.

Sailboats

A vessel under sail must display red and green sidelights, along with a sternlight.

Specifically:

- For any sailboat less than 20 m in length, the aforementioned lights can be combined into one all-round light to be displayed at or near the top of the mast;
- In addition to sidelights and a stern light, sailing vessels may also display two all-round lights near the top of the mast (an all-round red light over an all-round green light, to increase visibility). However, these cannot be used in conjunction with the combined all-round light as mentioned above; and
- Sailboats that are less than 7 m in length should exhibit these lights if practicable. Otherwise, there must be a flashlight or torch onboard which shows a white light. This light must be readily accessible to be used in time to prevent a collision.

Fishing Boats

Fishing vessels will display the following lighting configurations whether they are underway or at anchor:

- An all-round red light (green if the vessel is trawling) above an all-round white light in a vertical line, or an hourglass shape (i.e., two cones, one on top of the other, apexes pointing at each other); and
- If the vessel is underway, it will display normal lights for power-driven vessels underway, in addition to the requirements listed above.

Vessels Under Oars or Paddles

Vessels under oars or paddles, such as rowboats, canoes and kayaks, should exhibit at minimum a white light, while others are approaching. The white light can be in the form of a flashlight (electric torch) or lantern (i.e. that displays a white light) and be readily available to use in sufficient time to prevent a collision.

NOTE: *Canoes and other paddle craft sit very low in the water and have a round hull, which makes them more prone to swamping or capsizing. When operating a powerboat, reduce to no-wake speed when approaching a paddle craft in order to avoid capsizing it.*

Vessels at Anchor

Any anchored vessel of less than 50 m (164 feet) in length must display an all-round white light where it can be best seen, between the hours of sunset and sunrise.

Towboats

Lights that are required to be visible while any vessel is towing another vessel are sidelights, sternlights, and an all around white light on each end. However, sometimes towing vessels will tow multiple objects, such as barges, in a group. In this case, so long as the length of the group is less than 100 m (328 feet), there can be a single light at the end of the group.

Pleasure Craft Towing Another Boat

When a pleasure craft is towing another vessel that is in distress or in need of assistance, it must—in addition to using its regular navigation lights—take all possible measures to indicate that it is towing another vessel. Particularly, the pleasure craft should use a flashlight or other light source to illuminate the tow line.

Government or Police Vessels

Any government or police vessel that is rendering assistance or engaged in law enforcement duties will display a blue flashing light.

Vessels Being Pushed

In the waters of the Great Lakes Basin, vessels that are being pushed must exhibit a special flashing light at the forward end, in addition to sidelights and a sternlight. In other Canadian waters, a power-driven vessel that is pushing another must exhibit two masthead lights configured in a vertical line, as well as sidelights and a sternlight.

Sound Signalling Devices and Appliances

The following requirements for sound signalling devices and/or appliances apply to vessels operating on Canadian waters. These are used to alert other boaters of your presence, and to communicate your intentions during periods of reduced or restricted visibility.

A sound signalling appliance is fitted on the vessel and meets requirements as set out in the Collision Regulations. A sound signalling device is simply carried onboard—this can be an electric horn, a compressed gas horn, or a whistle.

- Vessels less than 12 m (39.4 feet) in length not already fitted with a sound signalling appliance must carry a sound signalling device such as a pealess whistle or a horn (electric or compressed gas).
- Vessels 12 m (39.4 feet) or more in length must carry a sound signalling appliance onboard.
- Vessels 20 m (65.6 feet) or more in length must have a fitted bell in addition to a whistle.

Radar Reflector

Pleasure craft less than 20 m in length or craft constructed primarily of non-metallic materials (wood or fibreglass), must be equipped with a passive radar reflector. This device will help the boat be seen by other boats that use radar detection. The radar reflector should be mounted properly as high as possible, and must be mounted or suspended at a height of not less than 4 m (13.1 feet) above the water if practicable.

A radar reflector is not required if:

- You only operate in limited traffic conditions, daylight, favourable environmental conditions and where compliance is not essential for the safety of the craft, or;
- The small size of the craft or operation of the craft away from radar navigation make compliance impracticable.

Other Navigation Aids

A magnetic compass can be used to help the operator of a pleasure craft measure a boat's heading, determine its course, and find directions. As a boater, however, you should note that a magnetic compass is influenced by the proximity of metallic and/or electrical devices. To avoid false information, ensure that your compass is mounted in an area free of magnetic and electrical interference.

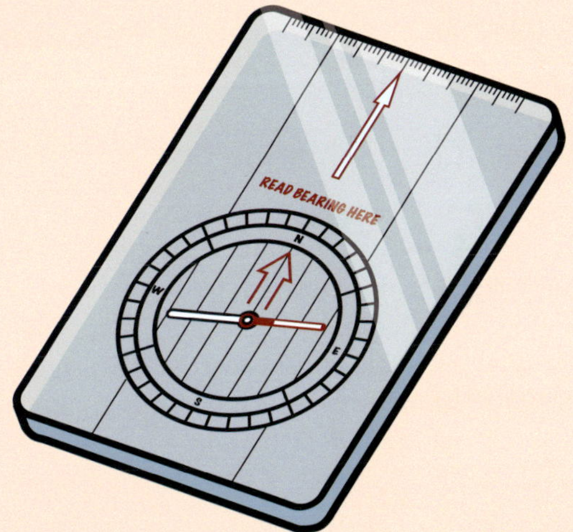

Nautical Charts (Marine Charts)

Today, there is a wide range of maps available for all uses. Outdoor enthusiasts can find topographical maps for mountain excursions as well as guide maps for lakes and rivers to plan expeditions. For boaters, maps are important too and are available as nautical charts which provide information on waterways. Nautical charts (marine charts) give useful information to boaters, especially on water depth, the type of bottom, the type of shoreline, current direction, coastal altitude, easily identifiable landmarks, and aids to navigation.

The Canadian Hydrographic Service publishes all nautical charts in Canada. For pleasure craft, large-scale maps (i.e. covering a small portion of the region) are often the most useful because of the high-level of detail they contain.

It is also important to check tides in tidal areas before heading out. The Canadian Tide and Current tables are also available from the Hydrographic Service. These tables can provide you with additional information such as the direction and times of flows as well as times of slack water.

Fisheries and Oceans Canada publishes a wide range of information charts to help boaters understand their nautical (or marine) charts. For example, Chart 1: Symbols, Abbreviations and Terms identifies the symbols, terms and abbreviations that boaters must use to interpret nautical charts published by the Canadian Hydrographic Service. Consulting and interpreting nautical charts is necessary in order for boaters to be aware of any underwater hazards.

To know which regional chart is most appropriate for your activity, consult the Canadian Hydrographic Service's Nautical Chart Catalogue. This catalogue is a large map showing the area covered by each available chart. To ensure that you are following that latest changes on routes, buoys, and water depths, be sure to keep your nautical charts up to date. The *Notice to Mariners* is frequently updated with the latest changes to nautical charts. Be sure to regularly check this notice, and to update your charts accordingly. For information on how to obtain charts, contact the Canadian Hydrographic Service at 1-866-546-3613, or visit *www.charts.gc.ca.*

Importance of the Nautical Chart to Boaters

Charts provide valuable information to boaters—detailed knowledge of waterways. In a rescue situation, using a nautical chart makes your task easier as a boater, because it:

- Helps identify a launch site.
- Shows the best route while considering currents, rapids, and other obstacles.
- Shows the location of waterways.
- Allows for an assessment of distances.

There is inevitably a sense of urgency when taking a distress call. Even though you will be in a hurry to help out, be sure to take the time to study a nautical chart. This may ultimately be what helps you successfully locate the scene of the boating accident.

Topographical maps are maps of the land areas depicting natural and artificial features of the land, including elevation contours, shoreline, rocks, as well as features above water including cultural features.

- They are intended primarily for the use of the general public on land.
- They are published by Natural Resources Canada and some provincial authorities.
- They are sometimes used when navigational charts are not available, but they usually do not depict underwater hazards, marine aids to navigation, channels, and anchorage areas, among other items.

Boat Traffic

There are 3 boat traffic zones:

1. Inshore Traffic Zones
Though all vessels are permitted to use these zones, they are generally used by vessels less than 20 meters in length or by sailing vessels.

2. Traffic Lanes
3 miles wide and normally only used by larger vessels, however, smaller vessels are also permitted in these zones.

3. Separation Zones (lines)
Separate boat traffic lanes going in opposite directions (similar to a highway median).

Additional Equipment Recommendations

For all boats, the previously described equipment is the minimum required. To respond effectively to a boating incident, the following additional items of equipment should also be carried onboard:

Emergency Kit:

- First-aid kit.
- Repair kit.
- One life buoy with 15 m buoyant heaving line.
- Two blankets.
- One flutter board.

Pyrotechnic distress signals, consisting of any of the following four types:

- Rocket parachute flares.
- Star rockets or shells that throw stars one or two at a time.
- Hand flares (limited visibility, because they are at water level).
- Smoke flares (flares that emit orange smoke and which are only effective during daylight).

In a distress situation involving a person who is in the water, ensure you have a method or equipment to get that person back into your boat. Consideration should be given as to how this will work if the person has sustained injuries.

As required, other equipment could be added to this basic material, including a pole or a communications system.

It could also include a magnetic compass to assist the operator in determining direction, but the operator must be aware of any nearby metallic or electrical devices, which are likely to distort readings from the compass.

Equipment Maintenance and Storage

A properly equipped boat will be of little use if the materials onboard are unusable because of breakage or early wear-and-tear. Maintaining and storing equipment not only makes sense aesthetically and economically, but the safety of boaters and their passengers depends on it. Equipment carried on the vessel must be stowed and readily accessible for immediate use if it is needed in an emergency.

Boating Equipment

Let's review the important parts of this chapter:

- Personal Flotation Devices (PFDs) and lifejackets can save lives and should be worn while boating whenever a vessel is in operation. If not worn, they must be readily accessible. Transport Canada requires that there be at least one approved PFD or lifejacket for each person onboard a vessel.
- Make sure your PFDs are in good condition before you go boating. Regularly check for rips and tears and replace them if damaged. Damaged PFDs or lifejackets are NOT considered approved. Also, make sure you are using the right PFD for the right activity.
- Safety equipment required onboard a vessel includes buoyant heaving lines, lifebuoys, re-boarding devices, manual propelling devices, anchors, bailers and manual water pumps, and fire fighting equipment.
- Marine radios, sound signals, flashlights and Emergency Position Indicating Radio Beacons (EPIRB) are all types of distress signals that can be used. By law, if you see a distress signal, you are required to render assistance where possible.
- Boat operators are required to ensure their vessel is equipped with the proper navigation lights when away from the dock between sunset and sunrise, and during periods of reduced visibility such as fog or rain.
- A sound signalling device is required onboard all vessels—this can be an electric horn, a compressed gas horn, or a whistle.
- Nautical charts published by the Canadian Hydrographic Service provide valuable information to boaters such as detailed knowledge of waterways. They can also be used to assist in responding to a distress call.

2

PRACTICE QUIZ

1. When is it most important that a power-driven vessel exhibit the proper navigation lights?

A. Whenever the vessel is docked

B. When away from the dock after sunset

C. When engaged in towing activities of any kind

D. When away from the dock after midday (noon)

2. Which of the following is a characteristic of a properly fitted Personal Flotation Device (PFD)?

A. It should be a relatively snug fit

B. It should rise above the ears and mouth

C. It should be very loose fitting

D. It should be uncomfortable

3. Which of the following equipment is required onboard ALL boats, regardless of size?

A. Lifting Harness

B. Anchor and 30 m of anchor cable

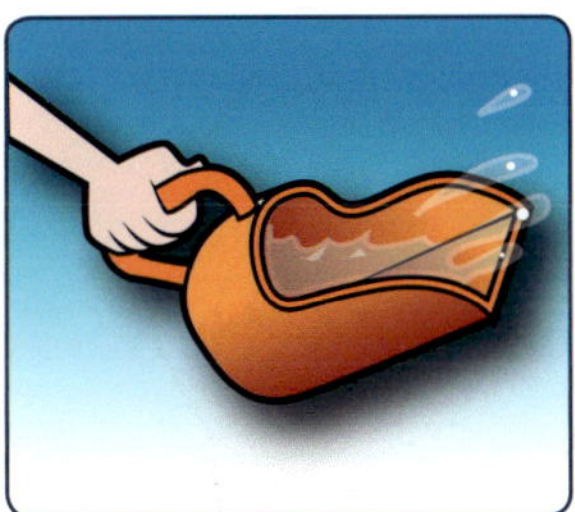

C. Bailer or bilge pumping arrangements

D. Cooking range or stove

4. What type of vessel is required to have a fire extinguisher?

A. Kayak

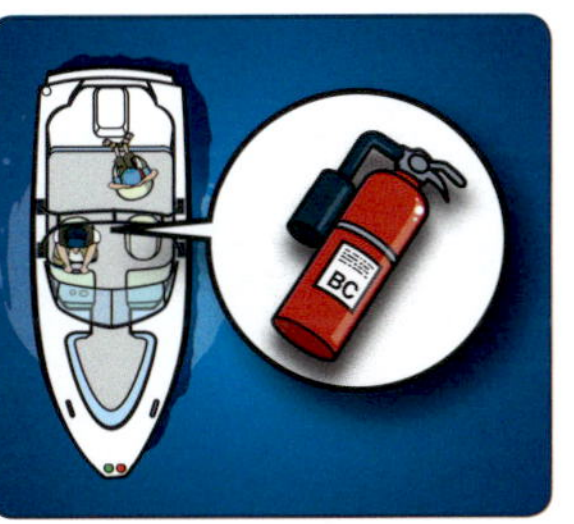

B. Powerboat

C. Rowboat

D. Sailing dinghy

Quiz Answers 1.b • 2.a • 3.c • 4.b

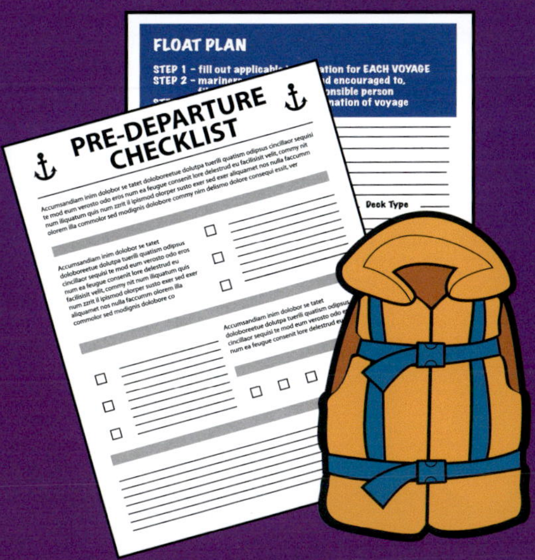

3. MINIMUM REQUIRED SAFETY EQUIPMENT

- → Minimum Equipment Required Onboard Vessels
- → Lifesaving Appliances
- → Boating Safety Equipment
- → Navigation Equipment
- → Fire Fighting Equipment

MINIMUM EQUIPMENT REQUIRED ONBOARD VESSELS

Different pleasure craft are required to carry different equipment, depending on the type and length of the boat, as defined in the Canadian Small Vessel Regulations.

There are two main categories of pleasure craft in these regulations:

- **Human-powered pleasure craft,** which include canoes, kayaks, rowboats, paddleboats.
- **Other pleasure craft,** which include all motorized vessels as well as sailboats.

Equipment that must be carried onboard a boat is separated into four distinct categories—lifesaving appliances, boat safety equipment, navigation equipment, and fire fighting equipment.

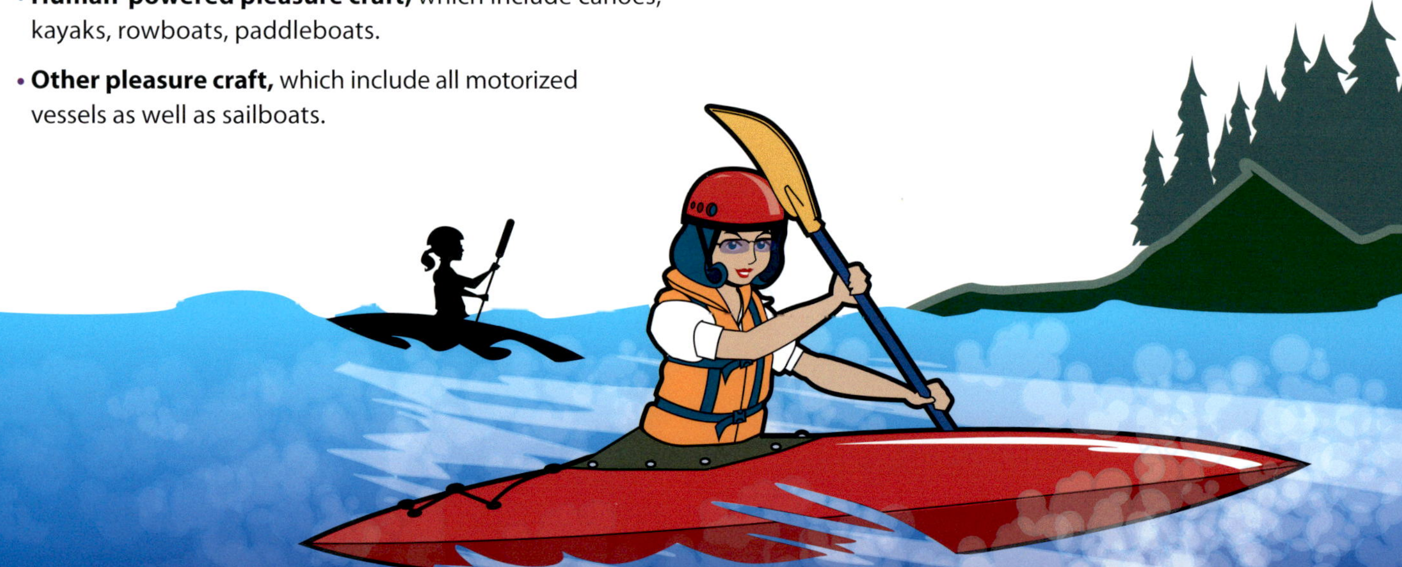

Lifesaving Appliances

Personal Lifesaving Appliances

Every pleasure craft, regardless of size, must carry the following equipment onboard:

A PFD or Lifejacket
A PFD or lifejacket for each person onboard (must be of an appropriate size).

A Re-Boarding Device
A re-boarding device if the boat has more than 0.5 m of freeboard.

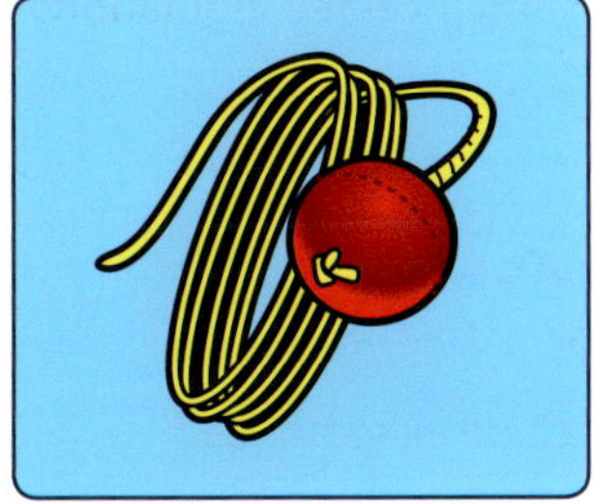

A Buoyant Heaving Line
Buoyant heaving line at least 15 m in length (however, a longer line is required for larger boats).

Additional Life-Saving Appliances

BOAT/VESSEL LENGTH	ADDITIONAL PERSONAL LIFE-SAVING APPLIANCES
Human-powered vessels and boats no longer than 6 m:	• Must have a buoyant heaving line at least 15 m in length.
Boats over 6 m up to 9 m:	• Must have a buoyant heaving line at least 15 m in length OR • An approved lifebuoy that is attached to a buoyant line at least 15 m in length.
Boats over 9 m up to 12 m:	• Must have a buoyant heaving line at least 15 m in length AND • An approved lifebuoy that is attached to a buoyant line at least 15 m in length.
Boats over 12 m up to 24 m:	• Must have a buoyant heaving line at least 15 m in length AND • An approved lifebuoy that is either attached to a buoyant line at least 15 m in length OR that is equipped with a self-igniting light.

Boats 24 m or longer:	• Must have a buoyant heaving line at least 30 m in length AND
	• A lifting harness with appropriate rigging AND
	• Two SOLAS-type lifebuoys:
	  • One that is attached to a buoyant line at least 30 m in length AND
	  • One that is equipped with a self-igniting light.

Lifesaving Appliances: Visual Signals

Depending on the length of the pleasure craft and area of operation, the following visual signals are required onboard (to be used as distress signals in the case of emergencies):

BOAT/VESSEL LENGTH	VISUAL SIGNALS
Boats no more than 6 m:	• Must carry a watertight flashlight OR • Three Canadian-approved pyrotechnic distress signals (flares), other than smoke signals.
Boats over 6 m up to 9 m as well as all human-powered vessels that are over 6 m:	• Must carry a watertight flashlight AND • Six Canadian-approved pyrotechnic distress signals (flares), other than smoke signals.
Boats over 9 m:	• Must carry a watertight flashlight AND • Twelve Canadian-approved pyrotechnic distress signals (flares), no more than six of which are smoke signals.

Exceptions to visual signal requirements:

Visual signals are not required onboard any boat that is not motorized and under 6 m in length. Pyrotechnic distress signals (flares) are not required on boats that:

1. *Are operating on rivers, lakes, or canals where the boat cannot be more than one nautical mile from shore OR*
2. *Do not have sleeping arrangements AND are engaged in (or preparing for) official competition.*

Boating Safety Equipment

Depending on the length of the pleasure craft, the following vessel safety equipment is required onboard:

BOAT/VESSEL LENGTH	BOATING SAFETY EQUIPMENT
Human-powered vessels:	• Must carry either a bailer OR • A manual bilge pump OR • Bilge-pumping arrangements.
Boats up to 9 m:	• Must have a bailer or a manual bilge pump AND • Either a manual propelling device OR an anchor that has at least 15 m of cable, rope or chain in any combination.
Boats over 9 m up to 12 m:	• Must have an anchor that has at least 30 m of cable, rope or chain in any combination AND • A manual bilge pump or bilge pumping arrangements.
Boats over 12 m:	• Must have an anchor that has at least 50 m of cable, rope or chain in any combination AND • Bilge pumping arrangements.

Exceptions to boating safety equipment requirements:

Bailers and manual bilge pumps are not required onboard vessels that cannot take on enough water to make them capsize, or if the boat has sealed compartments that are not readily accessible.

Navigation Equipment

Depending on the length of the pleasure craft, the following navigation equipment is required onboard:

BOAT/VESSEL LENGTH	NAVIGATION EQUIPMENT
Boats up to 9 m and all human-powered pleasure craft:	• Must have either a sound signalling appliance that meets the requirements of the Collision Regulations, or a sound signalling device AND • Navigation lights that meet the requirements of the Collision Regulations (only required if the boat is operated at night or during periods of restricted visibility) AND • A magnetic compass.
Boats over 9 m up to 12 m:	• Must have either a sound signalling appliance that meets the requirements of the Collision Regulations, or a sound signalling device AND • Navigation lights that meet the requirements of the Collision Regulations AND • A magnetic compass.
Boats over 12 m:	• Must have a sound signalling appliance that meets the requirements of the Collision Regulations AND • Navigation lights that meet the requirements of the Collision Regulations AND • A magnetic compass that meets the requirements of the Navigation Safety Regulations.

Exceptions to navigation equipment requirements:

A magnetic compass is not required if the boat is 8 m or less in length AND is operated within sight of navigation marks.

Fire Fighting Equipment

Fire extinguishers are required at the entrance or access to various spaces on the boat (such as accommodation space or machinery room). Depending on the length of the pleasure craft AND the types of appliances onboard the vessel, the following equipment is required onboard:

BOAT/VESSEL LENGTH	FIRE FIGHTING EQUIPMENT
Boats up to 6 m:	• Must have one 5BC portable fire extinguisher, only if the pleasure craft is equipped with: • An inboard engine OR • A fixed fuel tank OR • A fuel-burning cooking, heating, or refrigerating appliance.
Boats 6 m up to 9 m:	• Must have a 5BC portable fire extinguisher if the pleasure craft is power-driven AND • Must have an additional 5BC fire extinguisher if the pleasure craft is equipped with a fuel-burning cooking, heating, or refrigerating appliance.
Boats 9 m up to 12 m:	• Must have a 10BC portable fire extinguisher if the pleasure craft is power-driven AND • Must have an additional 10BC fire extinguisher if the pleasure craft is equipped with a fuel-burning cooking, heating, or refrigerating appliance.

BOAT/VESSEL LENGTH	FIRE FIGHTING EQUIPMENT
Boats 12 m up to 24 m:	• Must have a 10BC portable fire extinguisher at each of the following locations: • At each access to any space that is fitted with a fuel-burning cooling, heating or refrigerating appliance AND • At the entrance to any accommodation space AND • At the entrance to the machinery space (engine room). • One axe AND • Two fire buckets.
Boats 24 m or longer:	• Must have a 10BC portable fire extinguisher at each of the following locations: • At each access to any space that is fitted with a fuel-burning cooling, heating or refrigerating appliance AND • At the entrance to any accommodation space AND • At the entrance to the machinery space (engine room). • One power-driven fire pump located outside the machinery space, with one fire hose and nozzle capable of directing a jet of water into any part of the pleasure craft AND • Two axes AND • Four fire buckets.

Other Exceptions to Equipment Requirements

There are additional exceptions to required equipment for specific vessel types. Additional information on the following exceptions can be found in Section 2 Subpart 3, 4, and 5 of the Canadian Small Vessel Regulations.

Personal Watercraft

If all persons onboard the PWC are wearing a properly fitted, approved PFD or lifejacket, the PWC need only carry:

- A sound signalling device.
- A watertight flashlight or three pyrotechnic distress signals other than smoke signals.
- A magnetic compass (if it is operated out of sight of seamarks).
- Navigation lights that meet the requirements of the Collision Regulations if the PWC is operated at night or during restricted visibility.

Sailboards, Kiteboards, Paddleboats, Watercycles, and Sealed-Hull Sit-on-Top Kayaks

If every person onboard the pleasure craft is wearing a properly fitted, approved PFD or lifejacket, the only required equipment is:

- A sound signalling device.
- A watertight flashlight if operated at night or during periods of reduced visibility.

Racing Canoes, Racing Kayaks and Rowing Shells Engaged in Official Competition

Please refer to Small Vessel Regulations, Part 2 Subpart 5.

Onboard Required Equipment

Let's review the important parts of this chapter:

- Different pleasure craft are required to carry different equipment, depending on the type and length of the boat. The main categories of pleasure craft are: human-powered pleasure craft (canoes, kayaks, rowboats or paddleboats) and motorized vessels (including sailboats).
- Every pleasure craft, regardless of size, must carry a PFD or lifejacket of appropriate size for everyone onboard.
- A re-boarding device is required if the boat has more than 0.5 m of freeboard.
- Specific visual signals such as flashlights, pyrotechnics and smoke signals are required onboard in case of an emergency.
- Depending on the length of the pleasure craft, safety equipment such as bailers, bilge pump, manual propelling devices, anchors, ropes and chains, are required onboard.
- Specific navigation equipment such as sound signaling devices, navigational lights and a magnetic compass are required onboard.
- The length of the pleasure craft influences the fire fighting equipment that is required onboard. Ex.: 5BC portable fire extinguisher, 10BC portable fire extinguisher, axes and fire buckets.
- There are exceptions to required equipment for specific vessel types such as PWC, canoes, kayaks etc. Consult the Canadian Small Vessel regulations for additional exceptions.

1. Which of the following items is NOT considered fire fighting equipment?

A. A 5BC or 10BC fire extinguisher

B. An axe

C. A fire bucket

D. A watertight flashlight

2. Which of the following would meet visual signal requirements?

A. Carrying a watertight flashlight onboard

B. Raising and lowering outstretched arms

C. Hanging a white towel from the mast

D. Ringing a bell rapidly

3. Which of the following pleasure craft is NOT categorized as human-powered?

A. Canoes

B. Sailboats

C. Kayaks

D. Rowboats

4. What must be carried onboard a canoe with more than 0.5 m of freeboard?

A. A re-boarding device

B. A fire extinguisher

C. A cooking range

D. A lifebuoy

Quiz Answers	1.d • 2.a • 3.b • 4.a

4. TRIP PLANNING

- → Weather Conditions
- → Planning for your Trip
- → Boat Maintenance and Checklists
- → Load Capacities
- → Fueling Procedures

PLANNING FOR THE WEATHER

Checking the Weather Forecast

As a boater, you must check the local weather forecast before heading out in your pleasure craft. This can be done quite accurately and effectively by using the following sources:

- Newspapers.
- Radio.
- Television weather channel.
- Radiotelephones.
- Environment Canada.

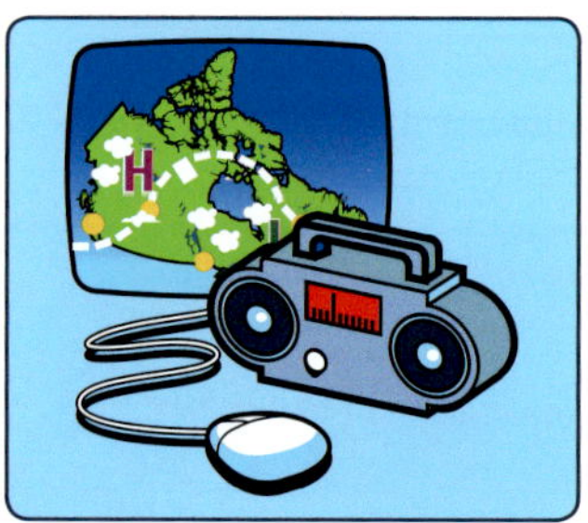

Weather forecasts may contain warnings on wind conditions that could be vitally important to boaters, specifically:

Strong Wind Warning

Sustained wind speeds in the range of 20 to 33 knots.

Gale Warning

Sustained wind speeds in the range of 34 to 47 knots.

Storm Warning

Sustained wind speeds in the range of 48 to 63 knots.

Hurricane Warning

Sustained wind speeds in the range of 64 knots or more.

Since weather conditions, particularly on the water, can change quickly, you need to be able to monitor your surroundings while out on the water so that you can anticipate and adapt quickly if necessary.

Specifically:

Keep an Eye on the Sky

Fog, dark clouds and lightning are obvious indications that bad weather is approaching.

Barometric Readings

A rising barometer usually indicates fair weather, while a falling barometer can indicate potentially foul weather.

Pay Attention to Shifts in Wind Direction and Temperature

These indicators suggest that foul weather could be imminent.

Look Westward

Foul weather tends to approach from the west (however, storms from the east tend to be more powerful).

Watch the Movement of Other Boaters and Monitor Radio and Weather Channels Frequently

Ask for recommendations via radio if you are in unfamiliar waters.

Preparing for a Storm

While boating, you and all your passengers should always wear a properly fitted Personal Flotation Device or lifejacket. If you encounter foul weather or another emergency, it will be one less thing to worry about.

If you encounter a strong wind warning or you feel there is an approaching storm (including sudden build-up of high waves), take the following steps to prepare:

- Your first priority should be to ensure that all passengers are wearing PFDs that are secured properly.
- Reduce speed and proceed with caution, watching for approaching boats and floating debris.
- Close all hatches and ports to avoid swamping.
- All passengers should sit low in the boat and near the centreline.
- Secure all loose items in the boat to avoid losing them overboard.
- Pump out bilges to keep the boat high in the water.
- Turn on navigation lights (if in conditions of restricted visibility).
- Check marine charts for the nearest shelter and note hazards.
- Head for the nearest safe shoreline.

When a Storm Hits

- If your boat engine stops, drop your anchor from the bow to combat drifting and swamping.
- Point the bow of the boat into waves at a 45-degree angle to keep your watercraft in the most stable position.
- If lightning is present, unplug all electrical equipment, remain low in the boat and away from metal objects.

Take note that after heavy rain, water levels can rise in streams, rivers or creeks, leading to an increase in debris on the surface of the water. Debris will usually accumulate close to shore, in inlets and under bridges. Try to avoid these areas if possible. Always proceed with caution after a storm.

Local Hazards

Boaters should always acquire local navigational charts to learn the types of hazards that can be found in the waterway, as well as the location of shipping lanes and other areas to avoid. When planning a route for your boating trip, plan it in such a way to avoid rapids or strong currents that could put your safety and that of your passengers at risk.

Trip Plans (Sail Plan)

Another useful safety measure to take before any boating trip is to file a trip plan (also known as a sail plan). Before heading out, the operator of a pleasure craft should complete a thorough trip plan and give it to a responsible person who is familiar with the instructions to follow in case of emergency. During your trip, this plan should be updated to avoid an unnecessary call for help. Preparing and sharing a trip plan can assist rescuers if it is necessary to initiate a call for search-and-rescue in case of emergency.

Your trip plan should contain the following information:

- Name and registration number of your craft.
- Type of craft (i.e., sailing or power-driven).
- Name, address and phone number of the watercraft owner.
- Number of persons onboard your vessel.

- Size, type and colour of your watercraft.
- Engine type (i.e., inboard, outboard).
- Distinguishing features of your craft.
- Type of radiotelephone and channel monitored.
- Safety equipment onboard.
- Emergency instructions.
- A trip description consisting of departure time, return time and proposed route.

Following your trip, be sure to contact the responsible person with whom your plan was filed, and inform them of your safe arrival home. This will prevent an unnecessary use of search and rescue resources.

NOTE: *See the quick reference guide on page 182 for a full trip plan and downloadable PDF.*

INSPECTION AND PREVENTATIVE MAINTENANCE

Boat Maintenance Schedule

Proper inspection and regular maintenance of your boat can extend its useful life and also help ensure that you and your passengers have an enjoyable, safe boating experience. An inspection should be performed, annually at the beginning of the boating season and also, before leaving the dock on every boating trip.

Engine

- Change the oil at least once every season (consult manufacturer's recommendations).
- Inspect belts and hoses before every voyage and replace those that are worn or torn.
- Check for corrosion and oxidation, and take preventive measures before they become potentially serious problems.
- Check and service your boat's transmission, and change fluids according to the recommended schedule.

Operating an Unseaworthy Vessel

Any person who knowingly operates or permits someone else to operate a vessel that is unseaworthy is guilty of an indictable offence and liable to imprisonment for a term of up to five years.

Pleasure Craft Courtesy Check Program

The Canadian Coast Guard Auxiliary, as well as other boating safety organizations, with the help of Transport Canada, offer free courtesy checks for pleasure crafts. During a courtesy check, a trained boating safety volunteer will board your boat to verify the safety equipment and other requirements, as well as identify any related safety issues.

These courtesy checks do not involve penalties. The goal is to educate boaters and prevent unnecessary emergencies on the water. It's a great opportunity for recreational boaters to learn more about boating safety and make sure that they are ready to head out on the water.

Visit Transport Canada's Office of Boating Safety website at *www.boatingsafety.gc.ca* for more information.

Pre-Departure Checklist

Another helpful tip for boaters is to complete a checklist of all required equipment and supplies prior to leaving the dock. The goal of this list is to make sure that the vessel is in good working order before every trip, ensuring that equipment works when needed to help avoid situations which could lead to unnecessary emergencies. Operators should instruct passengers about the use of all safety equipment when having a pre-departure meeting, before leaving the dock.

> **NOTE**: *See the quick reference guide on page 181 for a full pre-departure checklist and downloadable PDF.*

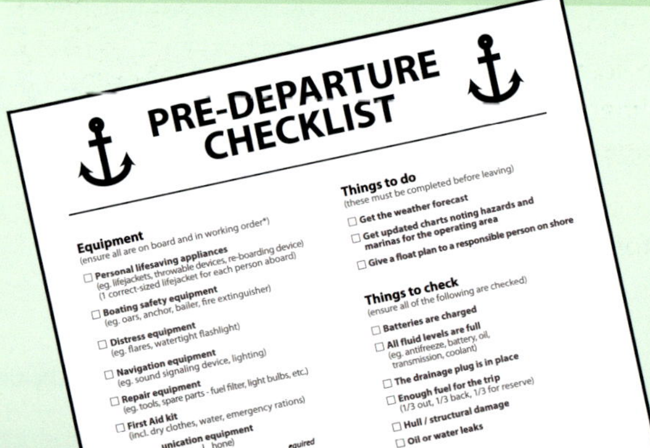

PRE-DEPARTURE CHECKLIST

Equipment
(ensure all are on board and in working order*)

- ☐ **Personal lifesaving appliances** (eg. lifejackets, throwable devices, re-boarding device) (1 correct-sized lifejacket for each person aboard)
- ☐ **Boating safety equipment** (eg. oars, anchor, bailer, fire extinguisher)
- ☐ **Distress equipment** (eg. flares, watertight flashlight)
- ☐ **Navigation equipment** (eg. sound signaling device, lighting)
- ☐ **Repair equipment** (eg. tools, spare parts - fuel filter, light bulbs, etc.)
- ☐ **First Aid kit** (incl. dry clothes, water, emergency rations)
- ☐ **…unication equipment** (… hone)

…equired

Things to do
(these must be completed before leaving)

- ☐ **Get the weather forecast**
- ☐ **Get updated charts noting hazards and marinas for the operating area**
- ☐ **Give a float plan to a responsible person on shore**

Things to check
(ensure all of the following are checked)

- ☐ **Batteries are charged**
- ☐ **All fluid levels are full** (eg. antifreeze, battery, oil, transmission, coolant)
- ☐ **The drainage plug is in place**
- ☐ **Enough fuel for the trip** (1/3 out, 1/3 back, 1/3 for reserve)
- ☐ **Hull / structural damage**
- ☐ **Oil or water leaks**

Your pre-departure checklist should include the following:

Personal Flotation Devices (PFDs) and/or Lifejackets

- At least one PFD per passenger and at least two PFDs total per watercraft.
- Inform all passengers where the PFDs are located and ensure children onboard are wearing their PFDs.

Sound-Producing Devices

- Horn, whistle or bell (at least two out of this combination) must be onboard.
- If a portable air horn is onboard, it should also include a spare can of compressed air.

Lights

- Ensure all required navigation lights are in working order.
- Check instrument lights.
- Ensure your boat is equipped with a flashlight.

Distress Signals

- Store flares in an accessible, dry location.
- Inform all passengers of signal location and use.

Docking and Anchoring

- Ensure the anchor is attached to the anchor line.
- Equip your boat with two fenders for docking.
- Inspect dock and anchor lines for wear and tear; replace if frayed.
- Equip your boat with two or three extra dock lines.

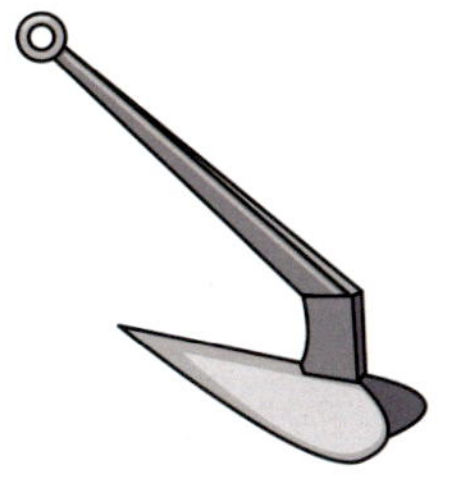

Documentation

- Keep your watercraft registration, radio license, fishing license and Pleasure Craft Operator Card (or proof of competency) onboard.
- Ensure local charts are on hand for quick reference.

Fire Extinguishers

- Store an approved fire extinguisher in an accessible place.
- Ensure mounts are secure.
- Inform all passengers of fire extinguisher location(s) onboard.

Tools and Spares

- Ensure your boat is equipped with a basic toolbox.
- Ensure you have important spare parts (e.g., fuel filter, light bulbs, etc.) onboard.

Emergency Boat Operation

- Inform all passengers of procedures for stormy weather or falls overboard.
- Learn how to operate the marine radio.
- Equip your watercraft with a first-aid kit, ensuring it is onboard and accessible.

Fuel and Oil

- Ensure all tanks are full.
- Check your boat's engine oil and coolant levels.

Ventilation

- On powered vessels, ensure interior spaces are well ventilated.
- If fumes are present after blowing, look for a leak or spill.

Weather Forecast

- Be sure to check the local weather forecast.
- Ensure you have a handheld radio to monitor local weather while out on the water.

Battery Care

- Ensure all powered equipment is working.
- Have spare batteries for accessories (e.g., handheld radio, flashlight, etc.).
- Ensure batteries are charged.

Bilges

- Clean bilge of any spills or waste.
- Ensure bilge is dry and pump is functional.

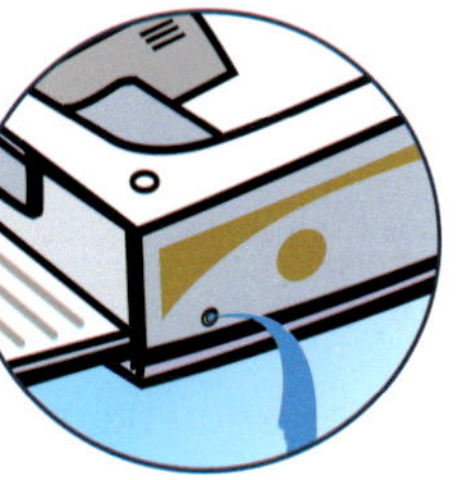

BOAT CAPACITIES

Engine Power and Load Capacity

As a boat owner or operator, you are expected to know the recommended gross load capacity that can be safely carried in the hull of your watercraft. Specifically, this:

- Includes the total weight of persons, equipment, stores, fuel, motor assembly and steering controls.
- Is indicated by the *equivalent number of adult persons*.
- Is indicated on a compliance notice which, if fitted, is permanently attached to the pleasure craft.

The compliance notice also indicates the recommended safe limits of engine power for the hull concerned. This recommendation is calculated based on the gross load capacity of the vessel.

Avoid Overloading and Overpowering Your Watercraft

An overloaded boat or overpowered boat can be extremely dangerous, and should be avoided at all cost. Either of these conditions may cause the vessel to sit lower in the water, making it susceptible to being swamped by its own wake or that of a passing boat.

Take extreme caution when loading your vessel, ensuring:

- That the weight of cargo and passengers are distributed evenly throughout the vessel; and
- The supplies are stored as low as possible in the boat.

Too much weight on either side could make your vessel less-stable and more prone to capsizing.

Fuelling Procedures

When mixed with air, gasoline evaporates quickly. Therefore, use caution when fuelling your boat. Remember that since gasoline fumes are heavier than air, they can accumulate in the hold (i.e., the bottom of your boat).

Observe the following procedures when fuelling your watercraft:

- Moor your boat.
- Do not smoke in fuelling area.
- Shut down all engines.
- Ensure that all persons not involved in fuelling the craft are ashore.
- Disconnect your vessel's fuel line and move your portable fuel tank ashore.
- If your craft has a fixed fuel tank, ensure all doors, windows and ports are closed, and electrical equipment is switched off.
- Place your onboard fire extinguisher within easy reach.
- While fuelling, ground the nozzle against the filler pipe to prevent a build-up of static electricity.
- Avoid overfilling the tank or splashing fuel.
- Close your vessel's fuel tank and clean up any spillage if necessary.

- Mix the oil and fuel in the tank, adding one and then the other (according to the watercraft manufacturer's recommended ratio).
- Replace the tank in the vessel and reconnect the fuel line (the tank should be securely fastened in the vessel as far from the motor as possible).
- Operate your vessel's engine compartment blower for **at least four minutes** immediately before starting up the gasoline engine.

The fuel tank should be kept away from sparks and heat and stowed in a well-ventilated location. Always store fuel in a clearly marked fuel container. Fuel tanks are red or orange for safety reasons. Other colours must not be used.

The One-Third Rule on Fuel Use

During any trip, it is always important to ensure you monitor your fuel supply. When operating a watercraft, always abide by the 1/3 Rule: use 1/3 of your fuel to operate; keep 1/3 of your fuel to get back to shore; and keep the other 1/3 as a reserve in case of emergency.

Fuel-Burning Appliances

There are many marine appliances that rely on propane or butane as a fuel source. These gasses can be more dangerous than gasoline on a boat, since many boaters do not understand the risks in using fuel-burning appliances. Like gasoline, propane and butane are heavier than air, and will quickly flow into the lower sections of your boat, and are highly explosive. Observe the following precautions when using fuel-burning appliances:

- Use fuel-burning appliances only in a well-ventilated area.
- Secure appliances in a manner that prevents fuel leaks.
- Keep gas cylinders and tanks in a secure, well-ventilated area.
- Follow all manufacturer's instructions.

Ignition Protection

Ignition-protected electrical devices are required onboard any boat that uses a gasoline engine or fuel-burning appliances. These are specially designed electrical parts that will not ignite gasoline fumes or propane fumes under normal conditions, by preventing sparks from escaping.

Always use marine-approved ignition-protected parts instead of automobile parts that do not offer this protection. If you are unsure if the parts on your boat are ignition protected, consult a qualified marine mechanic.

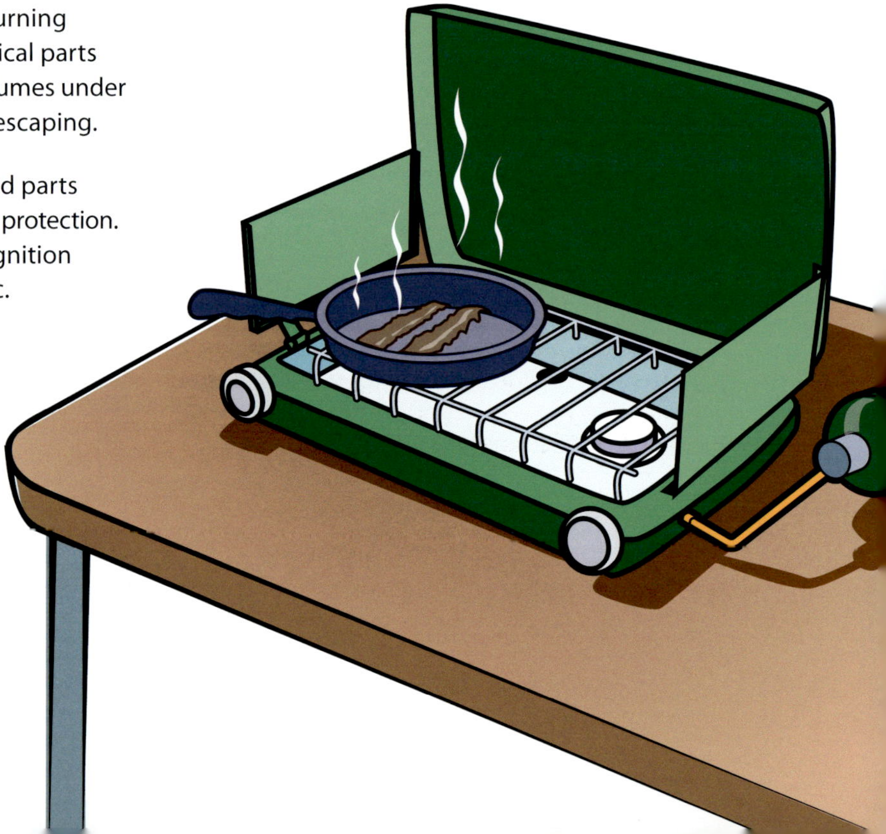

Trip Planning

Let's review the important parts of this chapter:

- Since weather conditions, particularly on the water, can change quickly, you need to be able to monitor your surroundings so that you can anticipate and adapt quickly if necessary. Particularly, if a storm is approaching.
- Before heading out, the operator of a pleasure craft should complete a thorough trip plan and give it to a responsible person ashore who is familiar with the instructions to follow in case of an emergency as well as helping ensure that you and your passengers have an enjoyable, safe boating experience.
- Regular maintenance, proper inspections of the boat and a pre-departure checklist will help to avoid situations which could lead to unnecessary emergencies.
- The compliance notice indicates the recommended safe limits of the engine power for the hull concerned. Take extreme caution when loading your vessel, ensuring the weight of the cargo and passengers are distributed evenly as not to swamp the vessel.
- The fuel tank should be kept away from sparks and heat and stowed in a well-ventilated location. Always store fuel in a clearly marked fuel container.
- During a trip, always monitor the fuel supply abiding by the 1/3 Rule: use 1/3 of your fuel to operate, 1/3 of your fuel to get back to shore and 1/3 as a reserve.
- Be aware of necessary precautions in responding to fires. Remember that fire needs three things: heat, fuel and oxygen. Removing any one of these three elements can extinguish a fire.

4

PRACTICE QUIZ

1. Which of the following are recommended sources of short-term and long-term forecasted weather information?

A. Friends or family members

B. Check local marine charts

C. Radio, TV or the Internet

D. Surveying the sky

2. Proper maintenance of a vessel has many benefits, including which of the following?

A. A greater boat buoyancy

B. An increase in wake

C. A safer boating experience

D. Improved towing capacity

3. **Which of the following is an accurate statement regarding a pre-departure checklist?**

A. They will help you avoid situations that lead to unnecessary emergencies

B. They are only to be used on long trips in unfamiliar waters

C. They are handy tools to help deal with emergencies

D. They are only to be used by the operator

4. **Under which circumstance may the Maximum Person Capacity of a vessel be exceeded?**

A. It may never be exceeded

B. If the weather forecast is favourable

C. If the vessel has a closed cabin

D. If there are extra life jackets onboard

Quiz Answers	1.c • 2.c • 3.a • 4.a

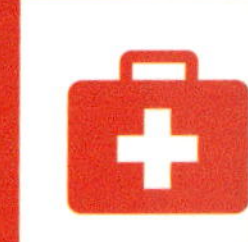

5. EMERGENCY PREPAREDNESS

- → Rendering Assistance
- → Responding to Emergencies
- → Responding to Cold Water Immersion
- → Medical Emergencies
- → Marine Communication Systems

RESPONDING TO EMERGENCY SITUATIONS

Rendering Assistance

All persons operating a vessel on Canadian waters are required to render assistance to all persons who are found at sea and in danger of being lost. If you see a distress signal, you are required to assist those in distress if you can do so without putting your vessel or crew at risk. If you cannot assist, make sure you immediately notify the nearest boaters or authorities who can assist.

When there is a risk of collision, operators of both vessels are required to render assistance until both vessels are out of danger.

Similarly, if two vessels collide, the operators must—to the extent to which they are not endangering their vessel, crew or passengers—render assistance that may be necessary to save them from any danger caused by the collision. They must stay by the other vessel until it has been determined that there is no further need of assistance.

Hull Leaks or Flooding

The following actions should be taken in response to a hull leak or flooding, such as when water is seen to be rising in a pleasure craft, or accumulating at the bottom of a craft:

- Locate the source of the hull leak or the flooding.
- Stop the leakage or the source of flooding if possible.
- Remove accumulations of water in the hold or other compartments of the pleasure craft by incorporating hand-held bailers, manually operated pumps or bilge pumping systems as appropriate to the circumstances and to the craft.
- Use or exhibit signals to indicate distress and need of assistance if necessary.

The operator of a pleasure craft should carry onboard at all times the tools and materials necessary to temporarily stop hull leaks or flooding.

Mechanical Breakdown

If you experience a mechanical failure or breakdown while operating your boat, remain calm and take the following actions:

- Alter your course and speed if necessary.
- Stop the vessel and drop anchor if necessary and where it is safe to do so.
- Investigate the source of the problem and correct it if possible.
- Use or exhibit signals to indicate distress and need of assistance if necessary.

5

FIRES

Fires

Gasoline fumes are extremely hazardous! Fuel and fumes onboard need only a single spark to cause an explosion or to start a blaze. Fires need three things: heat (e.g., a match or spark from the ignition), fuel (e.g., gasoline or propane) and oxygen. Removing any one of these three elements can extinguish a fire.

If your boat is underway and a fire starts:

- Stop the engine immediately, this should always be your FIRST action.
- Position your boat so that the wind will blow the fire away from your boat.
- Try to separate the fuel source from the fire.
- Take hold of your onboard fire extinguisher.
- Aim the extinguisher at the base of the fire.
- On the extinguisher, pull the pin and squeeze the two levers together.
- Use a sweeping motion with the extinguisher while maintaining focus on the base of the fire, continuing until the fire is completely out.

Collisions

If you are involved in a boating accident (i.e., involving injuries requiring medical treatment, incidents that result in death(s) or the disappearance of a person, or incidents involving property damage), you need to know what actions are required by law:

- Stop your vessel.
- Identify yourself and your boat.
- Provide assistance, if possible and warranted.
- Take down pertinent information with dates, time and conditions.
- File an accident report with the local law enforcement authority.

Failure to Stop at the Scene of a Collision

Vessel operators involved in an accident with another person or vessel are required to stop and provide their name and address. Failure to do this in a situation where any person has been injured or appears to require assistance is an indictable offence which may result in imprisonment for a term of up to five years.

In a case where the operator has knowledge that bodily harm has been caused to another person involved in the accident and fails to stop their vessel, the maximum sentence is increased to a maximum of ten years imprisonment.

Similarly, if the operator has knowledge that the accident has resulted in the death of another person involved and fails to stop their vessel, they may face imprisonment for life.

Capsizing, Swamping, Sinking or Grounding

The following actions should be taken in response to a pleasure craft that capsizes, swamps, sinks, or that runs aground:

- Ensure you are wearing your PFD or lifejacket.
- Stay with the craft when appropriate.
- Account for persons previously onboard the vessel in distress.
- Use or exhibit signals to indicate distress and need of assistance if necessary.

Falls Overboard

The major cause of fatalities involving small boats is drowning from a fall overboard. This is why it is important for boaters to wear their PFDs at all times. These falls overboard may have several causes, but are often the direct result of a vessel capsizing.

NOTE: *Many falls overboard that are not a result of capsizing occur when a person is standing on the boat's gunwale (side). Please use caution when on the water, and avoid standing on the side of your boat.*

If someone falls overboard:

- Stop your vessel if possible and throw something buoyant to assist the person overboard (this will also help briefly mark the spot if the person overboard submerges).
- Assign one person to keep sight of the overboard person and have them continuously point to the victim's location.
- Carefully manoeuver to recover the overboard person, ensuring (in the case of powerboats) that you keep them on the operator's side of the boat that is providing assistance.
- Establish contact with the overboard victim, using a buoyant heaving line or lifebuoy secured to the boat with a line.
- When attempting to recover the person overboard, be sure to first turn off your motor and ensure that the propellor has stopped.
- A heavy rope, chain or cable secured at both ends of the vessel and draped over the side (almost touching the water) can provide a makeshift step if no boarding ladder is available.

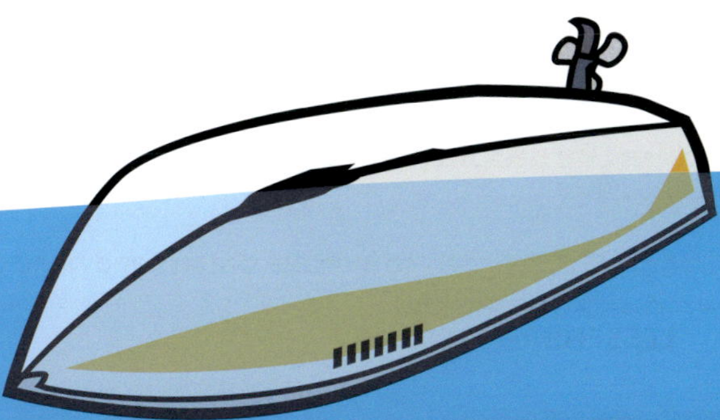

Cold Water Immersion

Many drownings and boating related fatalities are a result of cold water immersion. When a person falls into cold water, their body experiences a number of physiological responses which are affected by both the temperature of the water and the amount of time they are in the water. If a person overboard does end up in cold water, it is important to find a way to get them out of the water as soon as possible using whatever means available.

HEAT ESCAPE LESSENING POSITION

While wearing a PFD or lifejackets, some positions can help persons overboard to survive longer when immersed in cold water:

- If alone, adopt a fetal position by crossing arms tightly against the chest and by drawing the knees up close to the chest (this is known as the H.E.L.P. or heat-escape-lessening-position).
- If alone, climb onto a nearby floating object to get as much of the body out of or above the water.
- If in a group, huddle with other persons by getting the sides of everyone's chests close together, with arms around mid-to-lower back and legs intertwined.

HUDDLE TECHNIQUE

The following may provide additional protection to a person's body from hypothermia:

- Dry suit.
- Wet suit.
- Immersion suit.
- Survival suit.
- Exposure coverall.
- Multiple light layers of dry clothing.
- Water- or wind-proof outer layer.

NOTE: *Important! Wool is the best for all-around warmth. Wool, even when wet retains its insulation properties. Don't wear cotton, COTTON KILLS!*

Cold Water Immersion — Stages and Effects

Initial immersion — cold water shock

If a person falls into cold water, their body's initial reaction is a *gasp reflex* which can include hyperventilation and muscle spasms. This initial reaction is known as *cold water shock* and can result in water inhalation as well as significant changes in heart rate and blood pressure. These initial effects are present for the first two or three minutes of immersion into cold water that is 15°C or below. Cold water shock can lead to drowning and death. This is why it is very important to wear a proper PFD, especially when boating in cold water. If you do find yourself in cold water, try not to panic, focus on your breathing and try to take slow, deep breaths.

Short-term immersion — impaired function (swimming failure)
In cold water, you may begin to experience the loss of basic motor skills after only a few minutes. Between 10 and 30 minutes after immersion a person's hands quickly lose strength and sensation and subsequently their ability to swim (even strong swimmers). In cold water immersion cases, boaters often drown as a result of swimming failure before hypothermia ever has the chance to set in. Always wear a PFD when around cold water, and try to get your body out of the water as quickly as possible.

Longer-term immersion — immersion hypothermia
Following thirty minutes or more of immersion, hypothermia will begin to set in. Without intervention, the overboard person's overall body temperature will continue to drop until it reaches the temperature of the water.

MEDICAL EMERGENCIES

Hypothermia

Hypothermia is a drop in body temperature below normal level, which most frequently develops from exposure to very low temperatures such as immersion in cold water, exposure to cool air in water-soaked clothing, or prolonged exposure to low environmental temperatures.

Take the following actions to treat someone suffering from hypothermia or cold water shock:

- Remove the person from the source of cold exposure and provide dry shelter.
- If asked for, offer warm liquids but do not give alcohol or hot stimulants (such as coffee) to the person.
- Do not rub or massage the surface of the person's body or extremities.
- Use or exhibit signals to indicate distress and need of assistance if necessary.
- Seek medical help if necessary.
- If possible, prevent further decrease in body temperature and warm the person's body gradually by removing wet clothing and covering the person with warm dry objects, such as blankets or insulating devices.

The following signs and symptoms are exhibited in three stages as hypothermia progresses:

EARLY SYMPTOMS	INTERMEDIATE SYMPTOMS	FINAL SYMPTOMS
• Uncontrolled shivering • Slurred speech • Conscious but withdrawn	• Slow, weak pulse and respiration • Lack of coordination • Confusion and fatigue	• Weak, irregular or absent pulse and respiration • Lack of consciousness

Carbon Monoxide Poisoning

Carbon monoxide is an odourless, colourless gas that enters the bloodstream through the lungs and replaces the oxygen your body needs to survive. This deadly gas is produced any time a fossil fuel is burned. Sources on your boat may include gasoline engines, generators, cooking ranges, and space and water heaters. Prolonged exposure to low concentrations or very short exposure to high concentrations can lead to death.

Carbon monoxide can accumulate in the bilge, cabin or cockpit of your boat if you are operating at low speed with a strong tail wind, operating at higher speed with a high bow angle, idling the engine, or if your boat is next to another boat with an idling engine. There is also a high danger of poisoning if persons are swimming next to any idling vessel, or sitting on the rear swim step of an idling vessel.

To help prevent carbon monoxide poisoning, take the following steps:

- Keep air flowing through the vessel.
- Schedule regular engine and exhaust system maintenance inspections.
- Educate passengers about the symptoms of carbon monoxide poisoning.

- Assign an adult to keep watch when anyone is in the water.
- Install marine-approved carbon monoxide detectors in each accommodation space on your boat (be sure to check all detectors before each trip, and believe them if the alarm is activated). Carbon monoxide poisoning should be taken very seriously.

Do not confuse these symptoms as signs of seasickness or intoxication:

- Irritated eyes.
- Shortness of breath.
- Headache.
- Nausea.
- Weakness or dizziness.

If a person experiences any of these symptoms, take immediate action:

- Move the person to fresh air immediately.
- Investigate the source of carbon monoxide and correct it if possible.
- Use or exhibit signals to indicate distress and need of assistance if necessary.
- Seek medical help if necessary.

AVOID THESE DEATH ZONES!

Do not swim near or under the back deck, swim platform or in between pontoons. Carbon monoxide from exhaust pipes of inboard engines, outboard engines and generators builds up inside and outside the boat in areas near exhaust vents. STAY AWAY from these exhaust vent areas and DO NOT swim in these areas when the motor or generator is operating.

On calm days, wait at least 15 minutes after the motor or generator has been shut off before entering these areas. NEVER enter an enclosed area under a swim platform where exhaust is vented, not even for a second. It only takes one or two breaths of the air in this *death chamber* for it to be fatal.

SIDE VIEW: HOUSE BOAT

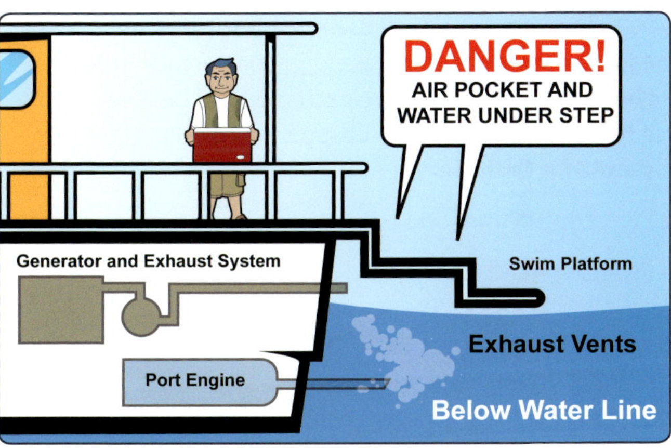

Heat Exhaustion

Heat exhaustion occurs when the body is unable to cool itself adequately. Usually this results from exercising in a hot, humid environment.

Symptoms include:

- Pale, cool, clammy skin.
- Profuse sweating.
- Muscle cramps/pains.
- Dizziness or light-headedness.
- Headache.
- Nausea.
- Elevated pulse.
- Elevated core body temperature (above 37°C).

If you suspect someone is suffering from heat exhaustion:

- Have the person rest in a cool area out of direct sunlight.
- Rehydrate the person with cool water or sports drinks.
- Loosen or remove clothing.
- Apply a cool compress to skin.
- Avoid giving alcohol or caffeinated beverages.

Heat Stroke

Heat stroke is a life threatening condition occurring when a person exhibits a dangerously high body temperature. Infants and the elderly are more prone to this, but healthy adults can also get heat stroke as a result of strenuous activity in a very hot environment.

Common symptoms:

- Flush, hot skin (moist in initial stages, dry in later stages).
- Dizziness, confusion or hallucinations.
- Elevated blood pressure (early stage).
- Shortness of breath or hyperventilating.
- Unconsciousness or coma.
- Core body temperature above 40°C.

Heat stroke is life threatening and should be taken very seriously. If you suspect someone is suffering from heat stroke, take them to a cool area and above all, seek medical help as soon as possible.

5

SEASICKNESS

Seasickness

Seasickness is a form of motion sickness that is experienced on the water.

Common symptoms include:

- Headache.
- Nausea.
- Vertigo.
- Pale, cool, moist skin.
- Weakness or dizziness.

If you experience seasickness, you can take the following steps to help minimize symptoms:

- Remain well hydrated.
- Avoid confined spaces, stay on deck in the fresh air if possible.
- Try to remain in the part of the boat that has the least amount of motion (usually the centreline).
- Focus on the horizon, occupying your mind with something other than the thought of being sick.

MARINE COMMUNICATIONS

The Maritime Communications System

In boating, many vessels are equipped with radios that operate through a maritime radio station or VHF Marine.

Radio airwaves in Canada are governed by Industry Canada. All radio operators must obtain a license from this department.

To operate a marine radio, you must first obtain a Restricted Operator's Certificate. You can do so by contacting Industry Canada and writing their Restricted Operator's Certificate examination.

To pass the examination, candidates must demonstrate that they:

- Are capable of operating modern VHF radiotelephone equipment.
- Possess a general knowledge of radiotelephone operating procedures and international regulations applicable to radiotelephone communications between stations, as well as those specific regulations relating to safety of life.
- Possess practical knowledge of the operation of Global Maritime Distress and Safety System equipment for vessels engaged on voyages within the range of VHF coast stations.

Calling for Help

If your vessel is in distress or in need of emergency assistance, you can use the VHF channel 16 on your radiotelephone, or call *16 from most cellphones. Channel 16 is reserved for emergencies only.

If you are in immediate danger (e.g. sinking or capsizing) use channel 16 and announce *mayday-mayday-mayday*. Provide your boat's name, your position, what the problem is, and the type of assistance required.

If you are not in immediate danger but need assistance (e.g. out of gas and cannot return to shore) use channel 16 and announce *pan-pan - pan-pan - pan-pan*. Provide your boat's name, your position, what the problem is and the type of assistance required.

Newer VHF radios usually come equipped with DSC (Digital Selective Calling) on Channel 70. This channel provides automatic digital distress alerts, which is a service provided by the Coast Guard on the East Coast, West Coast, Great Lakes and the St-Lawrence.

Limits of a Cellphone

Although a cellphone may be used to call for assistance, a VHF radio is still the preferred means of communication if available. Here are some of the limitations that make cellphones less reliable:

- They can often lose reception or can get wet and damaged easily when out on the water.
- Making a distress call will not alert nearby vessels that you are in danger, they could be the ones to help you if they could hear you.
- Some signals cannot be followed back to your location by rescuers.

Although it is not a good substitute for a marine radio, the Canadian Coast Guard Marine Communications and Traffic Services centre can be reached by dialling *16 or #16 on a cellphone. However, not all cellphone providers offer this service. Consult your cellphone service provider to see if this service is available for your phone.

Emergency Preparedness

Let's review the important parts of this chapter:

- → All persons operating a vessel on Canadian waters are required to render assistance to all persons who are found at sea and in danger of being lost. You are also required to assist those in distress if you can do so without putting your vessel or your crew at risk. If you cannot, you must immediately notify the nearest boaters or authorities who can.
- → Vessel operators involved in an accident with another person or vessel are required to stop and provide their name and address.
- → If a person falls into cold water, their body's initial reaction is a gasp reflex which can included hyperventilation and muscle spasms. This reaction is known as cold water shock. Cold water shock can lead to drowning and death. It is important to wear a proper PFD, especially when boating in cold water.
- → Carbon monoxide from exhaust pipes of inboard engines, outboard engines and generators builds up inside and outside the boat in areas near exhaust vents. STAY AWAY from these exhaust vent areas and DO NOT swim in these areas when the motor or generator is operating.
- → Heat exhaustion occurs when the body is unable to cool itself down. Know how to recognize the symptoms.
- → Heat stroke is a direct result of a high body temperature. Know the signs and seek medical help.
- → Seasickness is a form of motion sickness but on the water. Know how to recognize the symptoms.
- → Marine communications systems include marine radios and cellphones. It is important to know the capabilities and limitations of each.

1. **If you fall into cold water, in most cases you may only retain the motor skills needed to swim for about how long?**

A. 1 to 10 minutes

B. 10 to 30 minutes

C. 60 to 90 minutes

D. 90 to 120 minutes

2. **Which of the following is an early symptom of hypothermia?**

A. Shivering

B. Depression

C. Headache

D. Extreme hunger

3. Which of the following is an operator's FIRST priority if they are involved in an accident with another vessel?

A. Ensuring the anchor has been dropped before helping

B. Assessing property damages for insurance purposes

C. Making sure that no one has been hurt

D. Getting out of the other vessel's way

4. If a boat operator sees a distress signal, but is unable to provide assistance, what must they do?

A. Provide assistance even though it risks their own safety

B. Leave the area immediately and return to shore

C. Display an orange flag from the bow of their vessel

D. Notify the nearest boaters or authorities who can assist

Quiz Answers	1.b • 2.a • 3.c • 4.d

6. SAFE BOAT OPERATION & NAVIGATION

- → Positive Attitudes
- → Sound Signalling Devices
- → Nautical Charts and Publications
- → Navigation Rules and Regulations
- → Aids to Navigation

SAFE, RESPONSIBLE OPERATION OF YOUR WATERCRAFT

Proper Lookout

There are many distractions on the water while boating. As the vessel operator, it is your responsibility to monitor your surroundings constantly, including the boats around you, and at all times. You should assign another person on board to act as a lookout as well. Ensure no passengers or equipment can impede your line of sight. Scan the bow, starboard and port sides for boaters, swimmers, flags and floating debris. You are required to use every available means including radar and radio (if equipped) to determine whether there is any risk of collision with another vessel. This is not only common sense, it is the law.

Positive Attitudes

Operating a boat safely demands that operators develop alertness, judgement, caution and foresight.

Alertness

- Carefully monitor the surroundings.
- Observe and assess navigation conditions, weather changes and passengers' behaviour.

Judgement

- Assess whether the boat is adequate to meet the navigation conditions.
- Choose the best route.
- Operate your boat to suit weather conditions (e.g., slow down in bad weather).

Caution and foresight

- Assess the risks involved in each manoeuver.
- Plan what route to take.
- Accept your own limits as a boat operator.
- Be thoroughly familiar with your boat and its manoeuvering capacities (e.g., a pleasure craft travelling at high speeds requires more distance to stop in case of an emergency).

Safe Speed

All vessels should be operated at a speed that allows sufficient time and distance to take necessary action to avoid a collision. Obviously, different conditions and levels of expertise will warrant different speeds. Certain areas may enforce local speed limits. Check with your local boating authority before heading out on the water to determine speed limits (if any) in your area.

To determine a safe speed for your boat, take into account the following factors:

- Visibility conditions (e.g., fog, mist, rain, darkness).
- Wind, water conditions and currents.
- Traffic density, type of vessels in the area and their proximity.
- Vessel responsiveness (larger, more powerful boats require a larger turning radius and have a higher top end speed which requires more time and distance to stop).
- Proximity of any navigational hazards.

Also, remember that the wake generated by your vessel can cause damage to property and other watercraft. Adjust your speed accordingly.

BOATING SOUND SIGNALS

Sound Signalling Devices

The Canadian Collision Regulations require vessels to have an efficient means of producing sound signals based on the vessel's length:

- Vessels less than 12 m in length—Must have a whistle or other means of producing an efficient sound signal (such as an air horn).
- Vessel 12 m to less than 20 m in length—Must have a whistle onboard.
- Vessel 20 m to less than 100 m in length—Must have a bell onboard in addition to a whistle.

AIR HORN

Use of Sound Signals

Sound signals are used to indicate your intentions to other boaters. As a recreational boat operator, it is important to understand different sound signals, including what they mean and how to use them. When two power-driven vessels encounter each other within half a mile, sound signals must be used. The initiating vessel indicates a manoeuver, and the responding vessel agrees or disagrees.

SIGNAL	WHAT IT MEANS...
One short blast **Applies on the great lakes only*	I want to pass you on my port side (PORT = 1 syllable = 1 short blast).
One short blast **International rule 34(a)*	Altering course to starboard.
Two short blasts **Applies on the great lakes only*	I want to pass you on my starboard side (STARBOARD = 2 syllables = 2 short blasts).
Two short blasts **International rule 34(a)*	Altering course to port.
Three short blasts	Engine is in reverse.
Five short blasts	Danger, or do not understand approaching boat's intentions.
One prolonged blast (4–6 seconds)	Warning (entering or exiting a blind turn).
One prolonged blast every two minutes	Power-driven vessel operating in low or restricted visibility.
One prolonged blast plus two short blasts every two minutes	Sailing vessel operating in low or restricted visibility.

Use of Sound Signals in Restricted Visibility

During periods of restricted visibility, such as rain, mist, and heavy fog, you should slow your speed to give your vessel an opportunity to manoeuver should the risk of a collision arise. Sound signals are required during these conditions, to indicate your presence to other boats in the area.

WHEN VISIBILITY IS RESTRICTED BY FOG OR SMOKE, ADDITIONAL SOUND SIGNALS ARE REQUIRED:

VESSEL TYPE	SITUATION	SOUND REQUIREMENT
Power Vessel	Underway	Prolonged blast every two minutes.
Sailing Vessel	Underway	Prolonged blast + two short blasts every two minutes.
Power Vessel	Underway but not moving	Two prolonged blasts every two minutes.
Any Vessel	Anchored	Five seconds of rapid bell ringing every minute.
Any Vessel	Run aground	Three bell strokes + five seconds of rapid bell ringing + three bell strokes every minute.

Unless the risk of a collision is present, you should reduce your speed to the minimum required to remain on course.

NAUTICAL CHARTS AND PUBLICATIONS

To make navigation safer, regulations require operators of ships greater than 100 tons to have onboard the most recent editions of the required charts, documents and publications for the area in which they plan to boat.

If you are the owner or operator of a vessel less than 100 tons, you are not required to have the charts, documents and publications onboard as long as you have sufficient knowledge of the following:

- The location and character of charted shipping routes, lights, buoys and marks, and navigational hazards.
- The prevailing navigational conditions, taking into account such factors as tides, currents, ice and weather patterns.

BOATING RESTRICTION REGULATIONS

Federal Boating Restriction Regulations are specific to certain waters and waterways in Canada, and can specify:

- The types of vessels prohibited on a given waterway.
- Standardized speed limits on a given waterway.
- Maximum engine horsepower on a given waterway.
- Power vessel restriction on a given waterway.
- Waterskiing restrictions.

Other boating restriction regulations can also be passed and enforced by local municipal governments. Therefore, it is important to pay close attention to all signs encountered while boating, and to comply with any indicated regulations. Boaters must not tamper with or alter regulatory signs in any way (i.e., hiding, changing, damaging or destroying or mooring to a sign is not permitted). Failure to comply with these regulations is a chargeable offense.

OBEYING THE RULES OF THE WATER

Safe Boating to Avoid Collisions

Avoiding collisions involves precautionary measures (e.g., proper lookout, use of radar if present), but more importantly, collision avoidance is made possible when boat operators know how to deal with situations appropriately. Boats in constant motion will meet quickly, so take early and substantial action to avoid collisions.

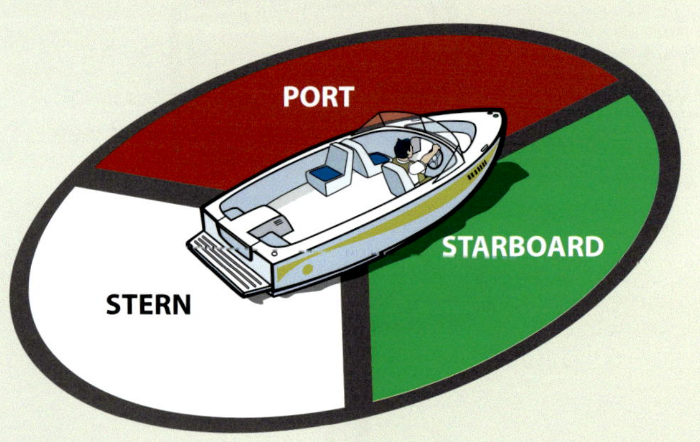

Definitions Relevant to Navigation Rules

Stand-On Vessel (A) —When encountering another vessel, as the operator of the stand-on vessel, you must:

- Maintain course and speed.
- Keep a proper lookout and return communication with the give-way vessel.
- Do all you can to avoid collision.

Give-Way Vessel (B)—As the operator of the give-way vessel, you must take early and substantial action to avoid collisions.

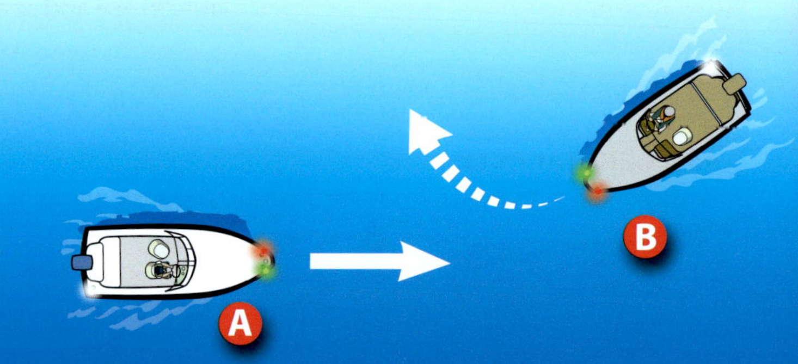

STERN

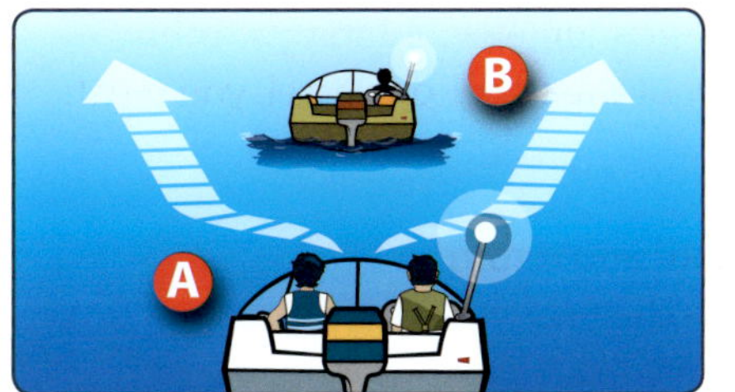

A is the give-way vessel.

STARBOARD

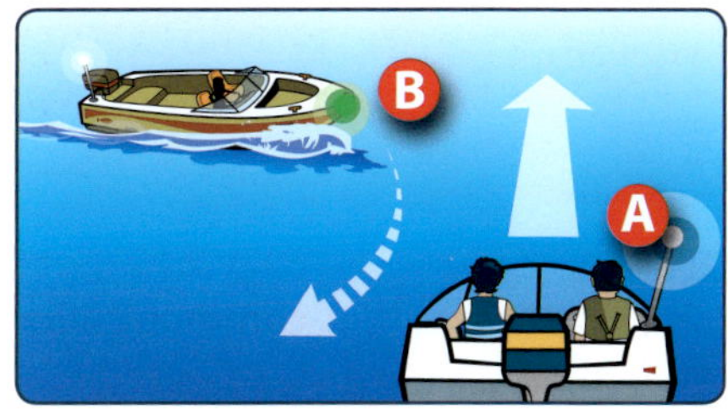

A is the stand-on vessel.

PORT

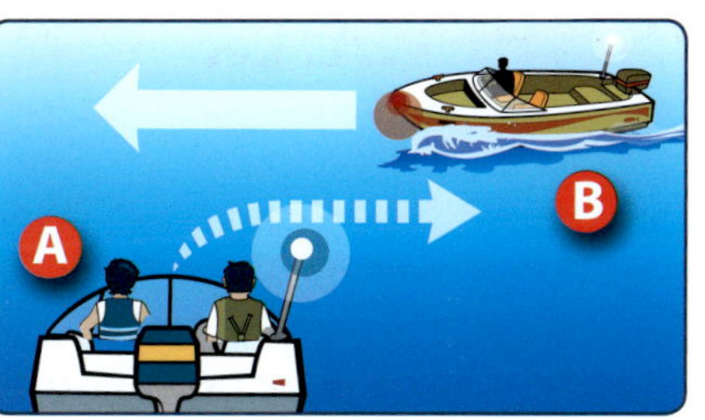

A is the give-way vessel.

Stern

If you are approaching any vessel from their stern (behind them), your vessel is the give-way vessel, keep out of its way.

Starboard

If you are approaching any vessel on their starboard side, your vessel is the stand on vessel. Maintain with caution your course and speed.

Port

If you are approaching any vessel on their port side, your vessel is the give-way vessel, keep out of its way.

AS A GENERAL RULE, *rowboats, sailing vessels and canoes are less manoeuverable and therefore have the right-of-way over power-driven boats. However, if one vessel is unable to manoeuver as it normally would, the most manoeuverable vessel gives way.*

Rules of the Road (Right of Way Rules)

The rules of the road in navigation are often similar to the rules on land. The Collision Regulations contain many rules pertaining to navigation; however, four rules are basic to navigation.

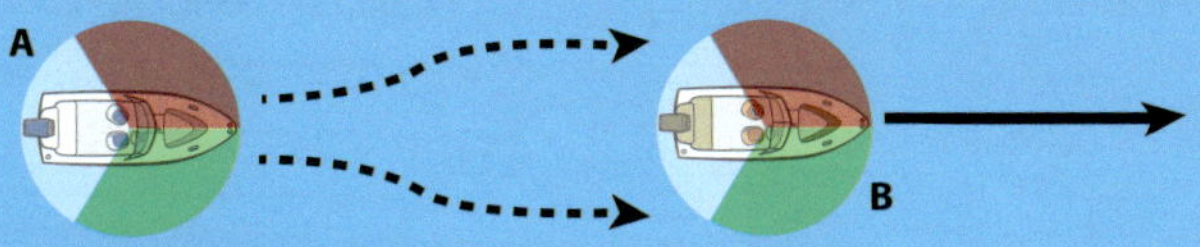

Overtaking - A boat that is overtaking another must steer clear of the overtaken vessel's path.

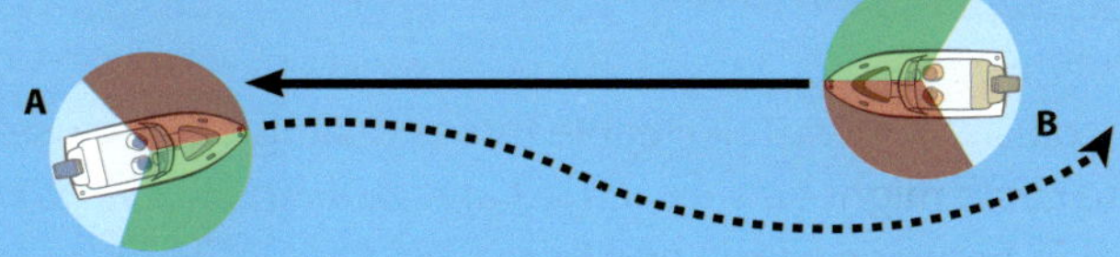

Port Approach - A vessel approaching from the port side must give way.

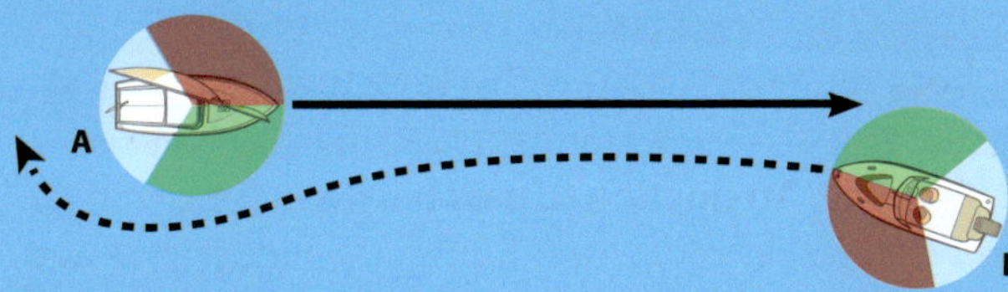

Sail-Boat Approach - As a general rule, rowboats, sailing vessels and canoes have the right-of-way over power-driven boats; however, if one vessel is unable to manoeuver as it normally would, the most manoeuvrable vessel gives way.

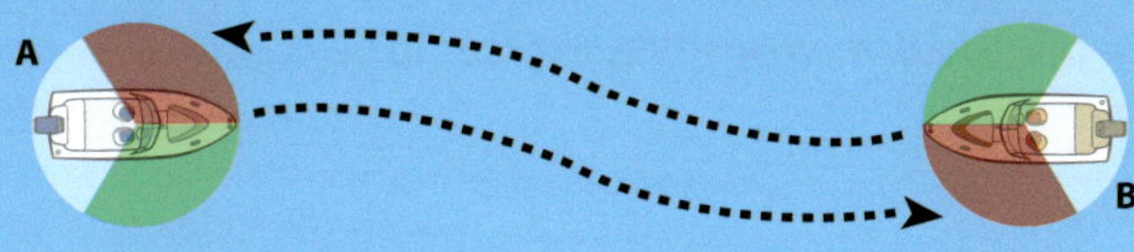

Head-On-Approach - When two vessels are heading toward each other, each must alter course and pass to the right of the other.

Operating Near Large Vessels

When operating near a shipping lane or in areas of high boat traffic, smaller craft are not easily visible to larger vessels. Always keep a lookout for larger vessels and be prepared to yield the right of way. Specifically, always steer well clear of vessels in tow, docked ferries, or ferries in transit. Be mindful of cable ferries pulling other vessels, the cable might be submerged and difficult to see. Do not get in between a ferry and its tow. Keep an ear out for one prolonged blast from a horn, as this may be indicating a departing dock.

NOTE: *Operators of smaller craft should attempt to travel in a group if at all possible, in order to be more visible.*

Vessels Not Under Command or with Restricted Manoeuverability

According to the Canadian Collision Regulations, any vessel not under command, or vessel restricted in its ability to manoeuver (including fishing vessels, sailboats, paddle craft, canoes and kayaks) has the right of way over power-driven vessels unless it is overtaking the power-driven vessel.

When possible, keep clear of large vessels such as commercial or shipping vessels. These larger vessels take a long time to adjust course and speed. Respect their space and give them a wide berth.

Steer Clear of Tug Boats

A tug boat can pull a vessel with a long tow line that can hang underneath the water's surface, making it very difficult to see. Attempting to pass between a tug and its tow could result in your vessel hitting the hidden line and capsizing, or getting hit by the towed object.

Shipping Lanes

Remember that larger vessels found in shipping lanes will not always see your small craft, making it very dangerous for a smaller vessel to enter a shipping lane. The Canadian Collision Regulations state that power-driven vessels less than 20 m in length, sailing vessels and manually-propelled vessels must all steer clear of and avoid crossing shipping lanes where possible. If you must cross a shipping lane, do so at a 90-degree angle, and only when it is safe.

Operation Within Narrow Channels

When approaching a narrow channel, stay to the starboard side and, using a prolonged blast, announce your approach to vessels that may be around the bend. When operating within a narrow channel, vessels must keep as near as is safe and practical to the outer limit of a narrow channel on their starboard side. Sailing vessels and vessels less than 20 metres in length cannot block the passage of a vessel that can safely navigate only within a narrow channel (i.e., recreational boaters travelling in a main channel should give way to larger vessels, such as tugboats).

AIDS TO NAVIGATION

In addition to their onboard equipment, boaters can rely on external aids to navigation. These are devices (buoys) or systems (collision regulations) which can help operators of pleasure craft determine their position and course. They also can warn of dangers or obstructions and advise operators of the best or preferred route.

NOTE: *It is important to be thoroughly familiar with the aids to navigation in your region.*

Port-Hand and Starboard-Hand Buoys

Port-hand buoys are green, and starboard-hand buoys are red. They show which side of a channel is safest to travel, and which side is hazardous. Generally, green buoys must be passed on the left side of a craft heading upstream (i.e., against the current). Red buoys must be kept on the right side of a craft when proceeding in the upstream direction.

Here's a simple way to help remember these rules: think of three **R's...**

RED TO THE RIGHT WHEN RETURNING

In many places, the direction of the current is determined by consensus or by the tide.

Port-Hand Buoys

- Are green in colour and can be shaped as cans, spars or pillars; mark the port (left) side of a channel or the location of a danger and must be kept on the port (left) side of a pleasure craft when proceeding in the upstream direction.
- Display identification letter(s) and odd number(s).
- If they carry a top mark, it is a single green cylinder.
- If they carry a light, it flashes green.
- If they do not carry a light, they each have a flat top.

Starboard-Hand Buoys

- Are red in colour and can be shaped as cones, as spars, or as pillars.
- Mark the starboard (right) side of a channel or the location of a danger and must be kept on the starboard (right) side of a pleasure craft when proceeding in the upstream direction.
- Display identification letter(s) and even number(s).
- If they carry a top mark, it is a single red cone pointing upward.
- If they carry a light, it flashes red.
- If they do not carry a light, they each have a pointed top.

Bifurcation Buoys

You may pass buoys with red and green bands on either side in the upstream direction. The main or preferred channel, however, is shown by the colour of the top-most band. For example, if a red band is on top, then you should keep the buoy on your starboard (right) side.

Special Buoys

Special buoys serve a variety of purposes. They are not primarily aids to navigation, but provide the boat operator with a host of information. Some are cautionary buoys to mark a firing range or seaplane bases, while others gather weather information, locate prohibited areas or mark designated mooring areas. The shape of the special buoys is not significant. They are identified by their symbols, drawings and colours.

Cautionary Buoys

- Mark an area where mariners are to be warned of dangers such as firing ranges, racing courses, seaplane bases, underwater structures, or areas where no safe through channel exists, as well as areas of traffic separations.
- Are coloured yellow.
- Display identification letters.
- If they carry a top mark, it is a single yellow *"X"* shape.
- If they carry a light, it flashes yellow every four seconds.

Anchorage Buoys

- Are used to indicate areas which are favourable for overnight anchoring.
- Are yellow in colour.
- Usually have an anchor symbol clearly visible on them.
- If they carry a light, it flashes yellow every four seconds.

Mooring Buoys

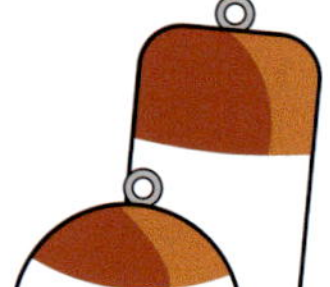

- Are used to moor or secure vessels.
- Are the only buoys to which you may legally tie your vessel.
- Usually are found in designated anchorage areas.

Swimming Buoys

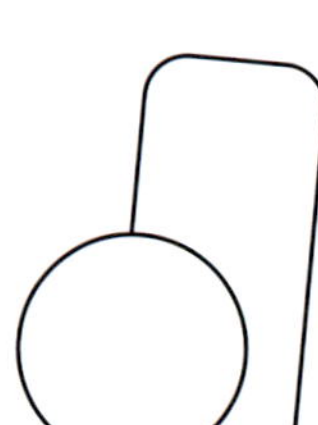

- Are used to mark the perimeter of a swimming area.
- Boaters should always stay clear of swimming areas and take extra care around swimmers.
- Are white in colour.
- If they carry a light, it flashes yellow every four seconds.

Diving Buoys

- Are used to mark an area where scuba or other diving activity is in progress.
- Are white in colour and carry a red flag not less than 50 centimeters square, with a white diagonal stripe extending from the tip of the hoist to the bottom of the fly.
- If they carry a light, it flashes yellow every four seconds.

Particular care must be taken when boating in waters where there are divers. A vessel engaged in diving must display a blue and white flag (International Code A Flag). A red and white flag carried on a buoy is used to mark areas where diving is in progress, although divers may stray from the boundaries of the marked areas.

Be sure you know what the diver down flags look like. If you see either flag, keep well clear of the vessel and diving site and proceed at a slow speed.

Control Buoys

- Are used to mark an area where boating is restricted.
- Are white in colour.
- Have an orange, open-faced circle on two opposite sides and two orange horizontal bands, one above and one below the circle.
- Have a black figure or symbol inside the orange circle indicating the nature of the restriction.
- If they carry a light, it flashes yellow every four seconds.

Hazard Buoys

- Mark random hazards such as rocks and shoals.
- Are white in colour.
- Have an orange diamond on two opposite sides and two orange horizontal bands, one above and one below the diamond symbols.
- If they carry a light, the light is yellow and flashes once every 4 seconds.

Information Buoys

- Display information of interest to boaters, by using either words or symbols.
- Are white in colour.
- Can be distinguished by the orange open-faced square symbol on opposite sides and the two horizontal bands, one above and one below the square.
- If they carry a light, it flashes yellow every four seconds.

Keep-Out Buoys

- Mark an area in which boats are prohibited.
- Are white in colour.
- Feature an orange diamond containing an orange cross on two opposite sides, and two orange horizontal bands, one above and one below the diamond symbols.

Day Beacons

Port-Hand Day Beacons

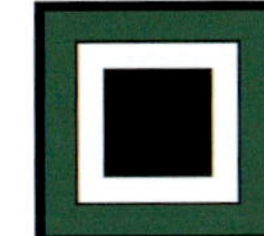

- Mark the port (left) side of a channel or the location of a danger during daylight hours.
- Must be kept on the port (left) side of a pleasure craft when proceeding upstream.
- Feature a square with a black or green coloured square, centred on a white background with a green reflecting border.
- May be numbered using odd numbers and be made of white reflecting material.

Starboard-Hand Day Beacons

- Mark the starboard (right) side of a channel or the location of a danger during daylight hours and must be kept on the starboard (right) side of a pleasure craft when proceeding upstream.
- Feature a black or red coloured triangle, centred on a white background with a red reflecting border.
- May be numbered using even numbers and be made of white reflecting material.

Junction Beacons

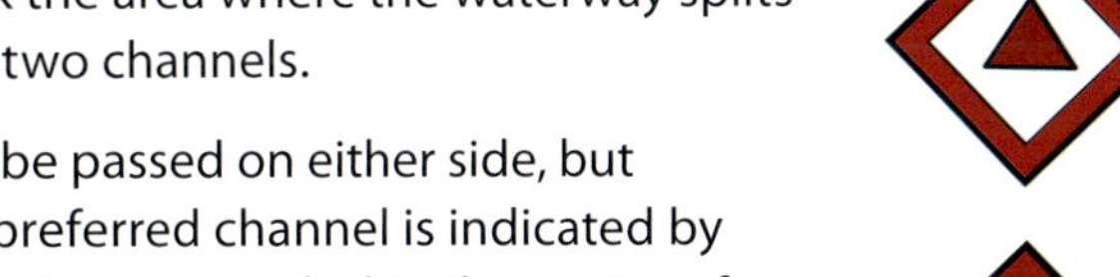

- Mark the area where the waterway splits into two channels.
- Can be passed on either side, but the preferred channel is indicated by the colour or symbol in the centre of the beacon.

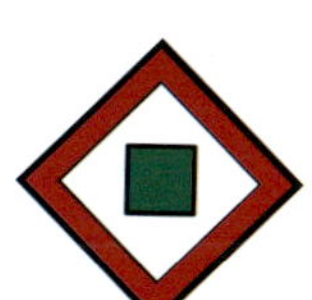

- Feature a red-outlined diamond with either a green square or red triangle in the centre, indicating the preferred channel.

Cardinal Buoys

- Feature four different types (north, south, east and west) and are used to indicate the location of safe water (i.e., a north cardinal buoy indicates that safe water is located to the north of it).
- Feature yellow and black coloration patterns, depending on the type of cardinal buoy.
- Are found primarily on international waterways and shipping lanes (in Canada, for example, they may be found on the St. Lawrence Seaway).
- Are generally used in conjunction with nautical charts to indicate a specific hazard.

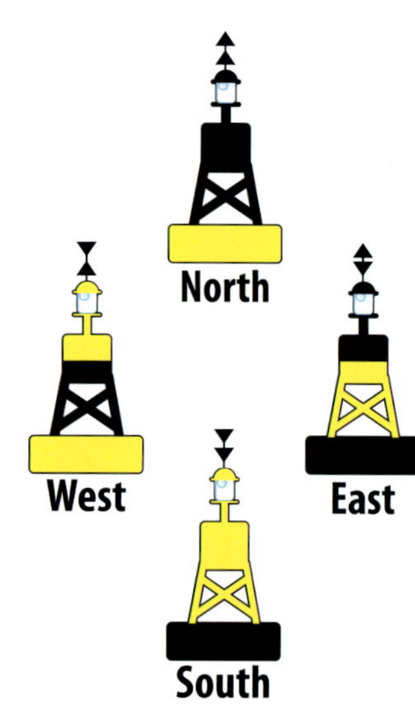

Isolated Danger Buoys

- Mark an isolated hazard in an area of water that is otherwise navigable.
- Are usually moored directly on or above the danger.
- Usually mark a large rock, shoal or sunken ship.

Tying Up to a Buoy

Pleasure craft operators may not interfere with marine signals, as stipulated in Section 439 of the Criminal Code of Canada, by:

1. Mooring the vessel to a signal, buoy or other sea-mark used for navigation; *OR*
2. Wilfully altering, removing or concealing a signal, buoy or other sea-mark.

NOTE: *Operators may only tie to mooring buoys.*

Safe Boat Operation & Navigation

Let's review the important parts of this chapter:

- As the vessel operator, it is your responsibility to constantly monitor your surroundings, including the boats around you, at all hours. Alertness, judgment, caution and foresight are crucial to safe and responsible operation of your watercraft.
- All vessels should be operated at a speed that allows time and distance to take necessary action to avoid a collision. Different conditions and levels of expertise will warrant different speeds.
- The Canadian Collision Regulations require vessels to have an efficient means of producing sound signals based on the vessel's length.
- The Rules of the Road, similar to right of way rules on land, are meant as a precaution for all boaters in avoiding collisions. Remember, the three R's, keep the **red** buoy to the **right** side of the boat when **returning** upstream.
- Always keep a lookout for larger vessels and be prepared to yield the right of way. Always steer clear of vessels in tow, docked ferries, or ferries in transit.
- Port-hand and starboard-hand buoys show which side of a channel is safest to travel, and which side is hazardous.
- Special buoys serve a variety of purposes. They are not primarily aids to navigation, but provide the boat operator with a host of information. They are identified by their symbols, markings and colours.

1. When coming around a bend in a narrow channel, what does one (1) prolonged blast emitted by Boat A using an efficient sound producing device indicate?

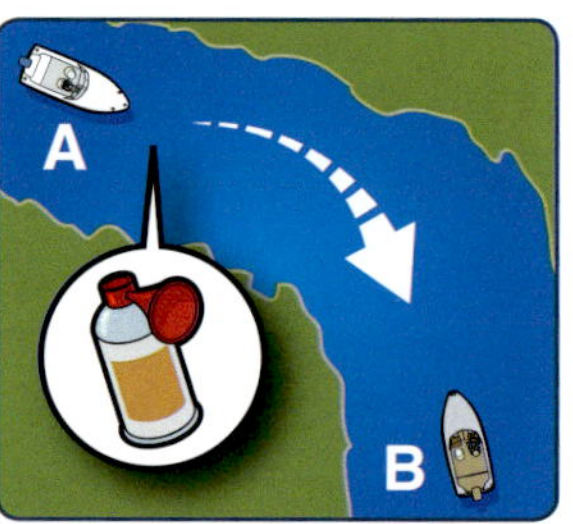

A. Its intention to turn right

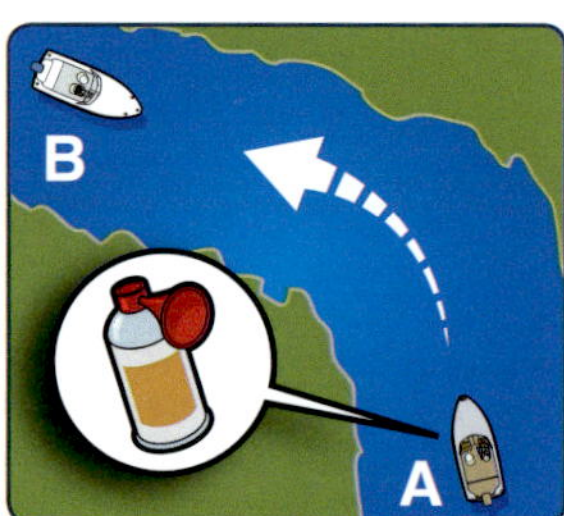

B. Its intention to turn left

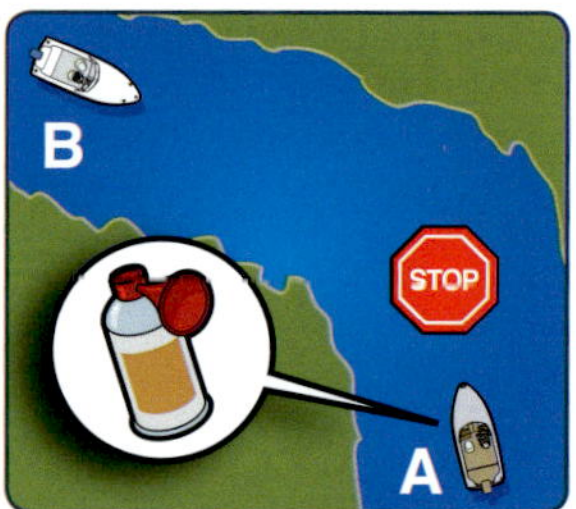

C. Its intention to stop

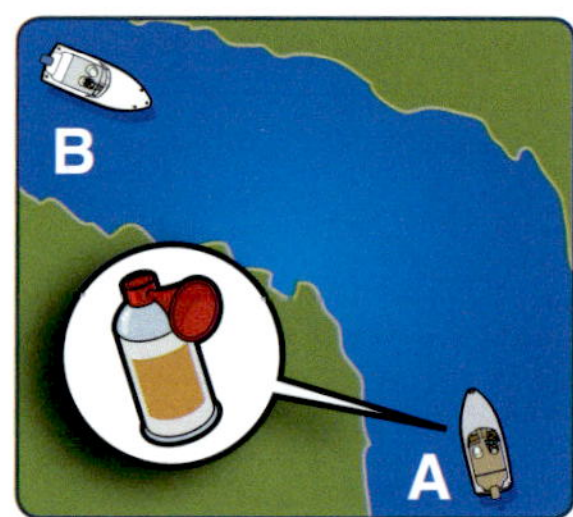

D. Its presence to other boats

2. As a recreational boat operator, what actions must you take when in a narrow channel?

A. Operate to your starboard side of the channel

B. Operate to your port side of the channel

C. Anchor at the entrance of the channel until clear

D. Operate near the center of the channel

3. If you encounter this red marker buoy when heading in the upstream direction (returning from sea), how should you proceed?

A. Keep the marker on your port (left) side

B. Keep the marker on your starboard (right) side

C. Pass on either side of the marker

D. Turn around; you may not proceed any further

4. Where can one find information on the location of charted shipping routes?

A. In local newspapers

B. On the Pleasure Craft Operator Card

C. On nautical charts and publications

D. On topographical maps of the area

Quiz Answers 1.d • 2.a • 3.b • 4.c

7. ENVIRONMENTAL LAWS & REGULATIONS

- → Towed Watersports
- → Disposal of Toxic Substances
- → Marine Sanitation Devices (MSD)
- → Pollutants
- → Aquatic Nuisance Species

OTHER PRECAUTIONS

Towed Watersports

Anyone who operates a vessel while towing a person on water skis or other device must also ensure that another responsible person is onboard observing or keeping watch of the person being towed. The person keeping watch must be able to relay information to the operator regarding the person being towed. Towing a skier without such a person onboard is illegal, and the operator may be found guilty of an offence punishable on summary conviction.

Additionally, it is illegal for the operator of a vessel to tow any person on water skis or any other device during the period from one hour after sunset until sunrise.

DISPOSAL OF TOXIC SUBSTANCES

As stated in the Canadian Regulations for the Prevention of Pollution from Ships and for Dangerous Chemicals, the dumping of oil, garbage, and other hazardous materials is illegal for commercial vessels and pleasure craft alike. Boat operators are not permitted to dump oil into the bilge of their boat without means for proper disposal. Oil and other chemicals must be kept onboard in a receptacle until they can be properly disposed of. If oil or other contaminants are discharged, this must be reported to the Coast Guard or government authorities as soon as possible. Any kind of spill or release of oil into the water may have serious long-term effects on the environment.

REGION	CONTACT NUMBER (TOLL-FREE)
Newfoundland and Labrador Region	1 (800) 563-9089 (24 hours)
Central and Arctic Region	1 (800) 265-0237 (24 hours)
Quebec Region	1 (800) 363-4735 (24 hours)
Atlantic Region	1 (800) 565-1633 (24 hours)
Pacific Region	1 (800) 889-8852 (24 hours)
Note: In all regions, marine pollution incidents may also be reported by contacting a MCTS centre on VHF channel 16.	

Marine Sanitation Devices (MSD)

The Regulations for the Prevention of Pollution from Ships and for Dangerous Chemicals do not permit the use of freestanding portable toilets onboard a vessel. All vessels fitted with a toilet must be equipped with a marine sanitation device or a holding tank to prevent pollution and discharge of raw sewage. The illegal discharge of untreated sewage can have devastating environmental effects and is a serious offence. A typical sanitation system consists of an installed toilet, a waste treatment system, and/or a holding tank. Marine sanitation devices are designed to treat sewage onboard the vessel, so that it may be discharged, as opposed to being kept in a holding tank.

For vessels with holding tanks, signs are displayed at marinas that have pump-out facilities. Check with local marinas to locate these stations prior to your voyage.

Pollutants

The following elements are officially considered pollutants and cannot be discharged in the waters of Canada:

- Hydrocarbons and any hydrocarbon composites (e.g., fuel, oil, plastics, etc).
- Toxic solutions or cleaning products.
- Gray or black water (e.g., dishwater, runoff from showers, bathtubs, etc.).
- Organostannic compounds (e.g., pesticides, herbicides, paint, etc.).
- Refuse materials (e.g., garbage or waste matter).

Avoid spreading these pollutants into Canada's waterways. Keep a trash container onboard and empty it when you get to shore. Before launching your boat, wash your hull, sanding or scraping any residue that might come loose into the water. Try to use alternative, organic (or *green*) cleaning products on and around your boat. These products are efficient yet environmentally sound and will not contribute to water pollution.

AQUATIC NUISANCE SPECIES

Non-native aquatic species, plants, fish and animals are invading Canada's waterways. These pests can propagate dramatically under the right conditions, displacing native species, clogging waterways, and affecting navigation and recreation. Once introduced, they are nearly impossible to eliminate. Hydrilla, Egeria Densa, Water Hyacinth and Zebra Mussels are all nuisance species that can be accidentally transported by recreational boaters when caught in propellers, intakes, or attached to hulls.

As a boater, you can help prevent the introduction and spread of non-native species from one body of water to another:

- Inspect your boat and dispose of any animals or aquatic plants prior to leaving any body of water.
- Flush raw-water cooling systems and clean sea strainers before moving your boat from one body of water to another.
- Empty bait buckets and remove any plant fragments from bait wells, fishing gear, trailers, dive gear or props, and dispose of them on land into a garbage receptacle.
- Drain all water from your bilge, motor and live wells.
- Wash your boat before putting it into a new body of water.
- Report new infestations of non-native aquatic species to Environment Canada.

Environmental Laws and Regulations

Let's review the important parts of this chapter:

- Anyone who operates a vessel while towing a person on water skis or other devices must also ensure that another responsible person is onboard observing or keeping watch of the person being towed.
- Dumping oil, garbage and other hazardous materials is illegal for commercial vessels and pleasure crafts alike.
- All vessels fitted with a toilet must be equipped with a marine sanitation device or a holding tank to prevent pollution and discharge of raw sewage.
- Hydrocarbons, toxic solutions, cleaning products, grey or black water, organostannic compounds and refuse materials are officially considered pollutants and cannot be discharged in the waters of Canada.
- Non-native aquatic species, plants, fish and animals can quickly spread under the right conditions, destroying native species, clogging waterways and affecting recreation in the area. Always inspect and wash your boat before launching and after retrieving your boat.

1. Which of the following is the best way to prevent the spread of aquatic nuisance species like zebra mussels?

A. Clean the boat at the boat launch

B. Let the boat dry on the ride home

C. Wait 5 days before re-launching your boat

D. Empty bait buckets after re-launching

2. Which of the following can cause serious, long-term environmental effects?

A. Having too many passengers on your boat

B. Using your boat every day

C. A small oil spill

D. Having an inboard engine

3. In which of the following circumstances is it REQUIRED to have a second person on the boat to act as a lookout?

A. When towing another person

B. When travelling in fog

C. When travelling at high speeds

D. Between sunset and sunrise

4. An oil spill must be immediately reported to which of the following authorities?

A. Local police department

B. The RCMP

C. Canadian Coast Guard

D. Nearest local marina

Quiz Answers	1.a • 2.c • 3.a • 4.c

8. BOATING RESTRICTIONS

- → Operator Responsibility
- → Restriction Signs
- → Boat Manoeuverability
- → Engine Noise Restrictions
- → Inspections of Pleasure Craft
- → The Effects of Drugs and Alcohol
- → Homeland Security Requirements in the United States

OPERATOR RESPONSIBILITY

As a responsible pleasure craft operator, it is important to remember that you share the waterways with others involved in many different and varied activities:

- Take extra care and stay clear of swimmers and swimming areas.
- Take extra care when near private property.
- Remember that every vessel is responsible for the effects of its wake—adjust the speed of your craft so that the wake and wave disturbance generated by the passage of your craft does not cause injury to persons, erosion of the shoreline or damage to others property.
- Know and obey Collision Regulations.
- Use courtesy and common sense to not create a hazard, threat, stress or an irritant to others, the environment or the wildlife.

One of the rules governing the operation of a vessel is that *every vessel is responsible for the effects of its wake*. Boat operators must ensure that the wake of their vessels does not endanger nearby boaters or cause property damage.

Boaters coming to help someone in distress must not compound the circumstances of an accident or, for that matter, cause another one. The effect of the boat's wake is extremely important when approaching the victim. Steps must be taken to ensure the wake is not so high that it washes over the victim.

Operator Fatigue

When a person has been on the water for a while, the motion of the boat along with noise, sun, glare and wind can lead to a case of operator fatigue. This is a condition in which the operator can no longer safely scan for hazards or react to hazards in a safe manner. Operator fatigue can be just as dangerous as operating under the influence of alcohol. Make sure you keep well-hydrated when out on the water. Know your limits and take frequent breaks to let your mind and body relax. Above all, avoid drugs and alcohol at all times while operating a boat.

Vessel Operation Restrictions

Vessel Operation Restrictions are specific to certain waters and waterways in Canada.

Universal Shoreline Speed Restriction

Certain provinces, such as Ontario, Manitoba, Saskatchewan and Alberta, have adopted speed limits of 10 km/h when craft are within 30 meters of the shoreline on all of their waters, whereas coastal provinces such as British Columbia and Nova Scotia have done the same for their inland waters.

Restrictions may also include:

- Prohibited vessel types on a given waterway.
- Standardized speed limits on a given waterway.
- Maximum engine horsepower on a given waterway.
- Power vessel restrictions.
- Towed watersport restrictions.

Vessel Operation Restrictions can also be passed and enforced by local municipal governments; it is therefore important to pay close attention to all signs encountered while boating.

How do you read a restriction sign?
There are five types of shapes for restriction signs. The frame colour is orange. Signs with a section with a green border indicate that a special condition applies to the restriction (e.g., the day or time that an activity is allowed).

The symbol on the sign indicates the type of restriction that applies. If the sign is arrow shaped, the restriction applies in the direction pointed by the arrow.

No internal combustion or steam engine is permitted

Power limit

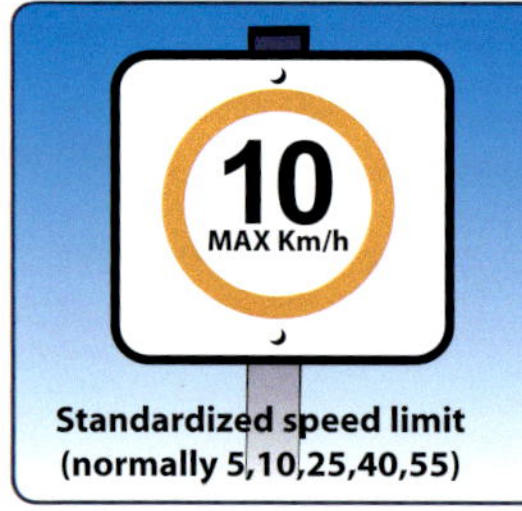

Standardized speed limit (normally 5,10,25,40,55)

No boats

No internal combustion or steam engine is permitted

No skiing north of the sign

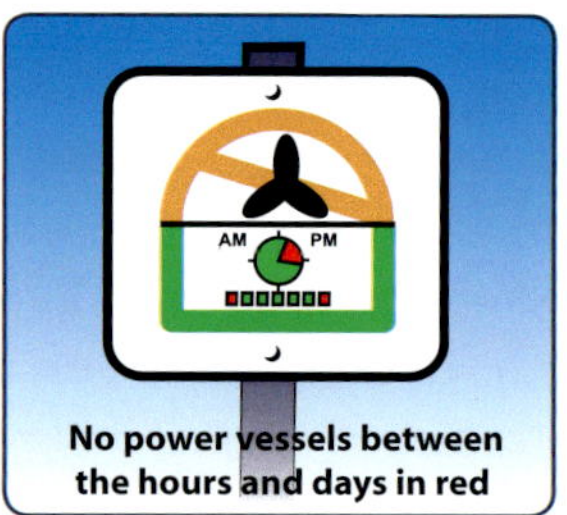

No power vessels between the hours and days in red

Boat Manoeuverability

All boats handle differently, and inexperienced operators need hands-on practice with a capable teacher to become proficient in handling their boat. A motorboat is most easily manoeuvered going against the current or wind. When moving with the current, the boat must be going faster than the speed of the current in order to maintain control and manoeuverability. Boats do not have brakes, so to reduce speed quickly, the motor should be put in reverse and power applied. Stopping in this manner requires practise. Consult your owner's manual for your boat and motor respectively for proper procedures.

Careless Operation

The offence of *Careless Operation of a Vessel* has been added to the Canadian Small Vessel Regulations. An operator who is doing any of the following could face charges or fines:

- Travelling in a way that could adversely affect the safety of people or property without considering the weather, boat traffic, hazards or potential hazards, or the number of people around the boat; or
- Operating a vessel in a careless manner without consideration for other people or for the factors listed immediately above.

Dangerous Operation

Operating a vessel in a dangerous manner is not only unsafe, it is illegal. Section 249(1)b of the Criminal Code of Canada says:

Everyone commits an offence who operates a vessel or any water skis, surf-board, water sled or other towed object on or over any of the internal waters of Canada or the territorial sea of Canada in a manner that is dangerous to the public, having regard to all the circumstances, including the nature and condition of those waters or sea and the use that at the time is or might reasonably be expected to be made of those waters or sea.

Everyone who commits an offence under this section may be sentenced to the following:

- Imprisonment for a term not exceeding five years.
- If the offence caused bodily harm to another person, the length of imprisonment may be up to ten years.
- If the offence caused the death of another person, the person who committed the offence is liable to imprisonment for a term of up to fourteen years.

Mufflers and Noise Levels

Any power-driven vessel that was manufactured after January 1, 1960 and operating within five nautical miles (9.26 km) from shore must be equipped with a muffler to reduce the noise level emitted from the engine.

This regulation does not apply to boats equipped with an unmodified outboard engine or any craft that is training, preparing for or engaged in an official competition.

Engine Noise Restrictions

It is illegal for a person to operate or give permission to operate a power-driven vessel unless the vessel has been equipped with a muffler to prevent excessive noise.

Exceptions to this rule include:

- Vessels built prior to January 1, 1960.
- Vessels practising for or engaged in official competitions.
- Vessels operating more than five miles from shore.

Inspections of Pleasure Craft

To verify and ensure compliance with the Small Vessel Regulations, an enforcement officer holds the right to inspect any vessel. This allows officers to:

- Board vessels.
- Examine vessels and their equipment.
- Request the owner or operator to provide them with personal identification, as well as any other relevant licence or document (including the Pleasure Craft Operator Card).

Additionally, an enforcement officer may, in the interest of public safety, direct or prohibit the movement of vessels or instruct operators to bring their vessels to a stop.

The following are among those designated as enforcement officers:

- Members of the Royal Canadian Mounted Police.
- Members of any harbour or river police force.
- Members of any provincial, county or municipal police force.

A vessel operator who, without reasonable excuse, fails or refuses to comply with a demand from a law enforcement officer to stop may face fines, as well as imprisonment for any subsequent violations.

DRUGS AND ALCOHOL

The Influence of Drugs and Alcohol on Boat Operation: Myths and Realities

Here are a few myths and realities about boating and alcohol:

MYTHS & REALITIES

"A few beers won't hurt."

REALITY Even in small amounts, alcohol affects coordination and judgment. A bottle of beer, a glass of wine or a drink of liquor all produce the same effect.

"Most drowning accidents result from swimming."

REALITY More than 60% of drowning accidents occur after the victim accidentally falls off a dock, shoreline or vessel into the water. Autopsies show that more than one-third of the victims of such falls (mostly men) were impaired by alcohol at the time of the accident.

Source: *Water and alcohol - myths and realities. Red Cross Society*

"Drinking alcohol while operating a boat is not a serious offense."

REALITY Operating a boat while intoxicated is just as dangerous as operating a car in that condition. The marine authorities are equipped with breathalyzers. If the results are positive, the operator could face charges.

"There's no harm in drinking alcohol on the beach before swimming."

REALITY Alcohol affects judgment. The person drinking can easily overestimate their abilities or misjudge a risk they would not take under normal circumstances. Furthermore, it is illegal to drink in some public places, such as a beach or a dock.

The Effects of Alcohol

Alcohol has the same effect on a boat operator as on a car driver. Here are a few examples:

Balance

Most people who die in a boating accident fall out of a vessel but not necessarily because it capsizes. Balance is one of the first faculties impaired by the very first drink of alcohol or the first beer.

Coordination

As the blood-alcohol level rises, people are less and less capable of coordinating their movements and reflexes. An intoxicated person will find it very difficult to swim or grab onto a lifebuoy, regardless of their ability when sober. Moreover, alcohol also affects vision.

Judgment and Sense of Risk

Most people lose their normal reasoning ability after just a few drinks. Under the influence of alcohol, the people may be inclined to take risks.

Blood-Alcohol Levels

The Criminal Code of Canada defines the legal limit for alcohol as 80 milligrams of ethyl alcohol per 100 milliliters of blood. This is also often expressed as 0.08 grams of ethyl alcohol per 100 milliliters of blood.

Anyone found operating a boat while disqualified, prohibited or under suspension is liable to additional criminal charges. Charges for these offences are listed under the Criminal Code of Canada and can include monetary fines, seizure of the vessel, imprisonment or others.

NOTE: *In some provinces, operating a pleasure craft while impaired could result in the loss of your motor vehicle driver's license.*

SECURITY CONSIDERATIONS

Homeland Security Requirements in the United States

If you plan on travelling to the United States by boat, you should be aware that the U.S. government has enacted specific measures since September 11, 2001, to help deter unlawful or dangerous operations on its waterways. U.S. Homeland Security Measures violations can result in severe consequences. Please be aware of the following measures and act accordingly to keep waterways safe and secure:

- Do not approach closer than 100 yards from all military, cruise-line, or commercial shipping vessels.
- Slow to *no wake* speed within 500 yards of any large U.S. Navy vessel.
- Observe and avoid all security zones.
- Avoid areas with military, cruise-line, or petroleum facilities.
- Observe other restricted areas near dams, power plants, or other facilities.
- Do not stop or anchor beneath bridges or in channels.
- Report any suspicious activity immediately to local authorities, the U.S. Coast Guard, or marine security personnel, or call the U.S. National Response Center's Terrorist Hotline at 1 (800) 424-8802.
- Do not approach or challenge those acting in a suspicious manner, and never confront the suspicious party.
- Ensure your boat is always locked and secured when unattended, and always take the boat keys with you.

For more information in port areas in the United States, call 1 (800) 682-1796, visit *http://www.uscg.mil*, or check with local authorities.

Propeller Intervention and Awareness

It is important to know the depth of the water where you are boating to avoid damage to the propeller. Also, be mindful that your propeller has the potential to injure people in the water.

Rotating at great speeds and with a lot of power, the potential danger posed by boat engine propellers should not be overlooked. Each year hundreds of people accidentally come into contact with moving propeller blades.

Since the propeller is located below the waterline and may be difficult to see, it is important that people are at all times aware of the propeller. This is most important when a person is in the water near the rear of a vessel or on the swim platform. As a precaution, operators should shut off the engine whenever a person is in the water within close proximity to their vessel.

Safety equipment is available and when used properly can significantly decrease the probability of a propeller strike.

Common examples of equipment are:

- Propeller guards.
- Ladder interlock kill switches.
- Man overboard cut-off switches.
- Lanyard engine kill/stop switches.

Boating Restrictions

Let's review the important parts of this chapter:

- Every vessel is responsible for the effects of its wake. Boat operators must ensure that the wake of their vessel does not endanger nearby boaters or cause property damage.
- There are five types of shapes for restriction signs. The symbol on the sign indicates the type of restriction that applies.
- Operating a vessel in a careless or dangerous manner is unlawful. An operator who is caught doing this could face charges or fines.
- It is illegal to operate a power-driven vessel that has not been equipped with a muffler to prevent excessive noise.
- To verify and ensure compliance with the Small Vessel Regulations, an enforcement officer holds the right to inspect any vessel.
- The effects of alcohol on an operator are amplified by heat and the movement of the boat. Specific factors such as balance, coordination, judgment and sense of risk are all impaired when under the influence of alcohol.
- Be aware of the Homeland Security Requirements in the United States and act accordingly to keep waterways safe and secure.

1. A motorboat is easier to manoeuver in which of the following conditions?

A. When travelling with the current

B. When travelling against the current

C. During a strong wind or storm warning

D. When most of the vessel's weight is at the stern

2. Boat operators are responsible for which of the following?

A. Any damage caused by their boat's wake

B. The condition of the local marina's facilities

C. The actions of other boat operators in the area

D. The approval of Personal Flotation Devices

3. Federal boating restriction regulations can specify which of the following?

A. The minimum number of people to carry onboard a boat

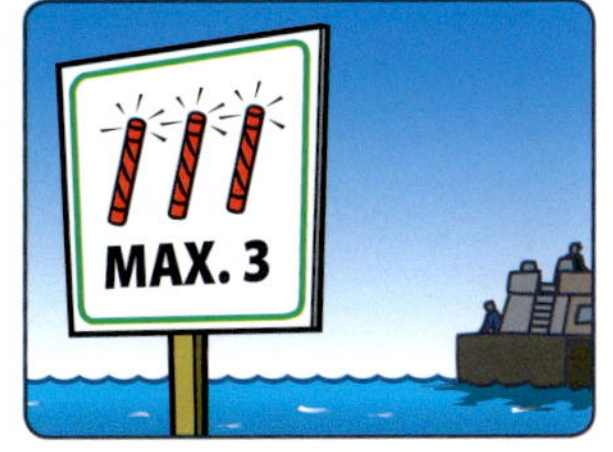

B. The maximum number of distress signals to carry onboard a boat

C. The types of vessels prohibited on a given waterway

D. The types of navigation buoys prohibited on a given waterway

4. Consuming alcohol or drugs before operating a boat increases the chances of which of the following?

A. A boating accident

B. Running out of gas

C. A false distress signal

D. An engine backfire

Quiz Answers 1.b • 2.a • 3.c • 4.a

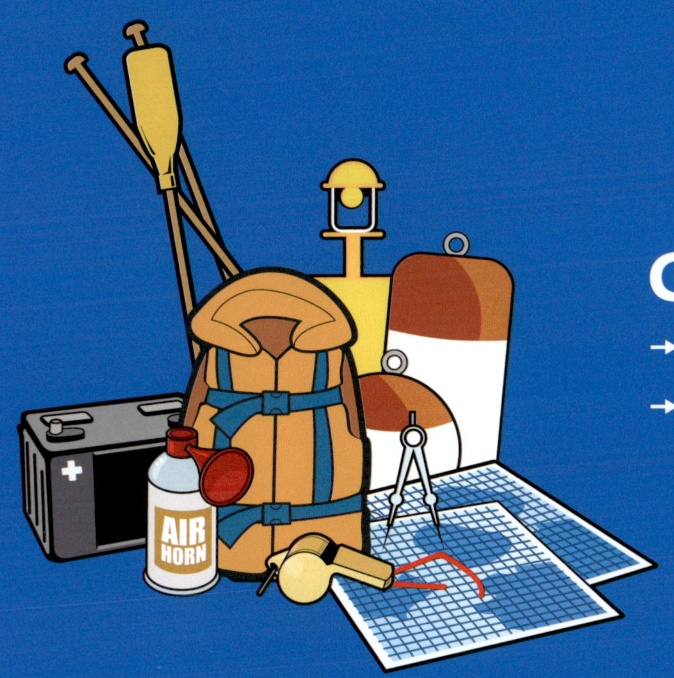

GLOSSARY

→ Quick Terms

→ Glossary

QUICK TERMS

Bow
The front part of the vessel.

Draft
The vertical distance from the waterline to the lowest point of the keel; the minimum depth of water in which a vessel will float.

Freeboard
The vertical distance from the waterline to the gunwale.

Give-Way Vessel
The vessel that must take EARLY and SUBSTANTIAL action to keep WELL clear of the stand-on vessel.

Hull
The body of a pleasure craft exclusive of masts, sails, rigging, machinery and equipment.

Lifejacket
Flotation device that is worn by a person, designed to hold the wearer's head out of the water, keeping them in an upright position. For a lifejacket to be Canadian-approved, it must be red, orange or yellow in colour.

Operate
The action of controlling the speed and course of a pleasure craft.

PFD (Personal Flotation Device)
Flotation device that offers less buoyancy than a lifejacket, and may not be designed to hold the wearer's head out of the water. No colour requirements to meet Canadian approval.

Pleasure Craft
A boat, a ship, a vessel, or any other description of watercraft that is used exclusively for pleasure and does not carry passengers or goods for hire, reward, remuneration or any object of profit.

Port
The left-hand side of the vessel looking forward.

Power-driven Vessel
Any vessel propelled by machinery as described in the *Collision Regulations*, rule 3.

Restricted Visibility
Any condition in which visibility is restricted by fog, mist, falling snow, heavy rainstorms, sandstorms or any other similar causes.

Sailing Vessel
Any vessel under sail, provided that propelling machinery, if fitted, is not being used.

Stand-on Vessel
When encountering another vessel, the stand-on vessel must:
1. Maintain course and speed.
2. Keep a proper lookout and return communication with the give-way vessel.
3. Do all it can to avoid collision.

Starboard
The right hand side of the vessel looking forward.

Stern
The back of the vessel.

Strong Wind Warning
A warning issued by Environment Canada when wind speeds are expected to be between 20 and 33 knots (37 to 61 km/h).

Vessel
Any type of watercraft, including non-displacement craft and seaplanes, used or capable of being used as a means of transportation on water.

Wake
The disturbed column of water around and behind a moving vessel which is set into motion by the passage of a vessel.

Waterline
The intersection of a vessel's hull and the water's surface.

GLOSSARY

A

ABOARD
To be in or on the vessel.

ADRIFT
Not moored or attached.

AFLOAT
A vessel that is not touching the ground and supported by water.

AFT
Towards the stern of the vessel.

AGROUND
Touching the bottom or ground.

AID TO NAVIGATION
Devices (buoys) or systems which can help operators to determine their position and course. They can also warn of dangers or obstructions and advise of the best or preferred route.

ALL-ROUND LIGHT
A light showing and unbroken light over an arc of the horizon of 360 degrees.

ANCHOR
A device used to hold a vessel in a particular location by attaching itself to the bottom.

ANCHOR LINE
A line attached to the anchor on one end and the vessel on the other.

ANCHORAGE
A designated area appropriate for daily or overnight anchoring of your vessel.

ASTERN
An area in back of, or behind the vessel.

B

BEACON
A man-made structure or sign built to be an aid to navigation.

BEAM
The greatest width of a vessel.

BEARING
The direction or position of an object, or the direction or movement, relative to a fixed point.

BIFURCATION BUOY
A buoy indicating the main or preferred channel where it divides.

BILGE
The lowest internal portion of the hull.

BLOWER
A mechanical device used to create a current of air used to blow any fuel vapours that may be trapped inside the bilge or engine compartment to the outside.

BOW
The front part of the vessel.

BRIDGE
The area from which the direction and movement of a vessel is controlled.

BUOY
An anchored float serving as an aid to navigation, to show reefs or other hazards, or for mooring.

BUOYANT HEAVING LINE
A line that is used to assist someone in distress. Must have the ability to float and consist of a single full length of rope of the appropriate length relative to your vessel and have a floating object attached to one end and be used only as safety equipment.

C

CABIN
An enclosed compartment of a vessel where passengers are carried.

CAN BUOY
A buoy that is painted green and marks the port side of the channel when returning from sea.

CAPSIZE
The overturning of a vessel.

CARDINAL BUOY
An aid to navigation used to indicate the location of safe water in relation to a cardinal direction (North, South, East or West).

CHART
Is a *road map* of a particular waterway that will provide all the necessary information required to safely navigate.

CLEAT
A T-shaped fixing on a vessel to which ropes or lines are attached.

COCKPIT
An area below deck level from which the tiller or wheel is handled.

COMPASS
An instrument that shows the direction of magnetic North.

COMPLIANCE NOTICE
A plate that is permanently attached to the vessel that contains information relating to the recommended grossload, maximum horsepower and maximum number of adult persons that must never be exceeded.

CURRENT
A body or flow of water moving in a definite direction.

D

DECK
The horizontal planks or platforms extended across the vessel to separate compartments.

DINGHY
A small boat that is often carried or towed by a larger vessel. A dinghy can also be a small racing yacht or recreational open sailing boat.

DISPLACEMENT HULL
A hull shape intended to move through the water rather than on top and supported only by buoyancy at any speed.

DOCK
1. A structure extending alongshore or out from shore to which vessels can be secured or moored.

2. An enclosed area of water for the loading, unloading and repair of vessels.

DOCKING
The process of approaching and securing a vessel to a dock or structure.

DOWNWIND
In the direction in which the wind is blowing; leeward.

DRAFT
The vertical distance from the waterline to the lowest point of the keel; the minimum depth of water in which a vessel will float.

DRIFT
To be carried by a current of water without propulsion.

E

EBB
The movement of the tide out to sea.

F

FENDER
A device used to protect the hull from damage caused by impact with other objects.

FLARE
Pyrotechnic distress signals used to indicate need of assistance.

FLUKE
The broad plate on the arm of an anchor that catches the ground.

FORWARD
The direction indicating the front or towards the bow of a vessel.

FREEBOARD
The vertical distance from the waterline to the gunwale.

G

GALE WARNING
Sustained wind speeds in the range of 34 to 47 knots.

GIVE-WAY VESSEL
The vessel that must take EARLY and SUBSTANTIAL action to keep WELL clear of the stand-on vessel.

GROUNDING
To touch or touching the bottom or shore.

GUNWALE
Upper edge of a vessel's side.

H

H.E.L.P.
Heat Escape Lessening Position. Fetal position to help prevent body heat from escaping when immersed in cold water.

HATCH
An opening in the deck of a vessel for access to the interior.

HEADING
A direction or bearing in which a vessel is pointing.

HELM
A tiller or wheel and any related equipment for steering and controlling a vessel.

HULL
The body of a pleasure craft exclusive of masts, sails, rigging, machinery and equipment.

HULL SPEED
Also referred to as displacement speed, is the maximum speed at which a displacement hull can operate.

HURRICANE FORCE WIND WARNING
Sustained wind speeds in the range of 64 knots or more.

HYPOTHERMIA
Is a drop in body temperature below normal level, which most frequently develops from exposure to very low temperatures.

I

INBOARD
Towards the centre or middle of a vessel.

K

KEEL
The structural centreline at the bottom of a vessels' hull.

KNOT
1. A unit of speed that equals 1 nautical mile (1.85 km) per hour.
2. A fastening by tying a piece of rope in tucks and loops.

L

LATITUDE
The angular distance of a point either north or south of the earth's equator.

LIFEBUOY
A buoyant life preserver in the shape of a ring that can be thrown to a person in distress.

LIFELINE
A coated wire that is fastened around the deck to prevent passengers from falling overboard.

LIGHT WINDS
Wind speeds less than 15 knots.

LOAD
The total weight of persons, equipment, stores, fuel, engine assembly and steering controls recommended for a vessel.

LOCK
A short confined section of a waterway in which the water level can be adjusted to raise or lower a vessel.

LONGITUDE
The angular distance of a point either East or West of the meridian at Greenwich, England.

M

MASTHEAD LIGHT
A white light placed over the vessel's front and rear centreline, showing an unbroken light over an arc of the horizon of 225 degrees toward the front of the vessel.

MAYDAY
An international radiotelephone distress signal used to indicate urgent need of assistance.

MODERATE WINDS
Sustained wind speeds in the range of 15 to 19 knots.

MOORING BUOY
A permanently anchored buoy to which a vessel can be secured.

N

NAUTICAL MILE
A measurement of distance defined as 1.85 km.

NAVIGATIONAL RULES
The governing regulations and laws as they relate to the navigation of vessels.

NAVIGATIONAL AID
Equipment onboard your vessel used in navigation. E.g. compass, GPS.

O

OPERATE
The action of controlling the speed and course of a pleasure craft.

OPERATOR
The individual in care and control of a vessel.

OUTBOARD MOTOR
A motor that is on the outside of a vessel.

OVERBOARD
Over the side of a vessel into the water.

OVERTAKING
To catch up with and pass another vessel while traveling in the same direction.

P

PCOC (Pleasure Craft Operator Card)
Pleasure Craft Operator Card is proof of operator competency as it relates to the safe operation of a recreational powered watercraft.

PFD (Personal Flotation Device)
Flotation device that offers less buoyancy than a lifejacket and does not turn the wearer face up out of the water. PFDs are now available in a variety of colours.

PLANING HULL
A hull shape intended to move above the water rather than through and supported only by dynamic forces of motion.

PLEASURE CRAFT
A boat, a ship, a vessel, or any other description of watercraft that is used exclusively for pleasure and does not carry passengers or goods for hire, reward, remuneration or any object of profit.

PORT
The left-hand side of the vessel looking forward.

PORTHOLE
A small exterior window or opening on a vessel.

POWER-DRIVEN VESSEL
Any vessel propelled by machinery as described in the *Collision Regulations*, rule 3.

PRE-DEPARTURE CHECKLIST
A checklist of all required equipment and supplies to complete prior to departure.

PROPELLER
A device for propelling a vessel, consisting of a revolving shaft with two or more blades.

PWC (Personal Watercraft)
A small, jet-powered craft.

R

RE-BOARDING DEVICE
Is a ladder or other device used to assist a person who is in the water to get back into the vessel. Is required when the freeboard is 0.5 meters or greater.

RIGGING
The system of ropes, cables or chains used to support and control a vessel's masts and sails.

RIGHT OF WAY
The privilege of a vessel to navigate in front of another vessel.

RODE
The combination of rope and chain used to attach the anchor to the vessel.

ROWBOAT
A small boat propelled by oars.

RUDDER
The underwater portion of a vertical piece hinged near the stern of a vessel used for steering.

S

S.O.S.
An international code signal of distress produced by signalling three short blasts, three long blasts, followed by three shorts blasts. (dot-dot-dot, dash-dash-dash, dot-dot-dot)

SAFE SPEED
A speed that allows effective care and control of a vessel, allowing sufficient time and distance to avoid a collision.

SAILING VESSEL
Any vessel under sail, provided that propelling machinery, if fitted, is not being used.

SEAWORTHY
A vessel in good condition and able to operate on the water.

SECURE
Fixed or fastened so as not to become loose.

SHOAL
An area of shallow water as a result of hidden underwater danger.

SIDELIGHTS
A green light on the starboard side and a red light on the port side, each showing an unbroken light over an arc of the horizon of 112.5 degrees on their respective sides.

SIGNAL
A gesture, action, or sound that is used to convey information.

SLACK WATER
The state of the tide when it is turning and has ceased to ebb and is about to flood.

STARBOARD
The right hand side of the vessel when looking forward.

STAND-ON VESSEL
When encountering another vessel, this vessel must:

1. Maintain course and speed.
2. Keep a proper lookout and return communication with the give-way vessel.
3. Do all it can to avoid collision.

STERN
The back of the vessel.

STERN LIGHT
A white light placed as nearly as practicable at the stern, showing an unbroken light over an arc of the horizon of 135 degrees, toward the rear of the vessel.

STORM WARNING
Sustained wind speeds in the range of 48 to 63 knots.

STRONG WIND WARNING
A warning issued by Environment Canada when wind speeds are expected to be between 20 and 33 knots (37 to 61 km/h).

SWAMP
To fill or become overwhelmed with water.

T

THROTTLE
A device used in regulating the flow of fuel or power to an engine and therefore controlling the speed.

TIDAL CURRENT
A current created as a result of tidal action.

TIDE
The alternate rising (flood) and falling (ebb) of the sea due to the gravitational pull of the moon and sun.

TILLER
A horizontal handle attached to the rudder used as a lever for steering.

TOPOGRAPHICAL MAP
Is a map showing physical surface features of land using contour lines to represent variations in elevation.

TOWING LIGHT
A yellow light having the same characteristics as a sternlight.

TRIP PLAN
A record that details the planned itinerary of a voyage and is filed with a responsible person on shore.

V

VESSEL
Any type of watercraft, including non-displacement craft and seaplanes, used or capable of being used as a means of transportation on water.

VHF RADIO
Very High Frequency radio used to communicate over long distances. Radio Operators Certificate is required to use a VHF radio.

W

WAKE
The disturbed column of water around and behind a moving vessel which is set into motion by the passage of a vessel.

WASH
The disturbed water left behind a moving vessel.

WATERLINE
The intersection of a vessel's hull and the water's surface.

WIND DIRECTION
The direction from which the wind originates.

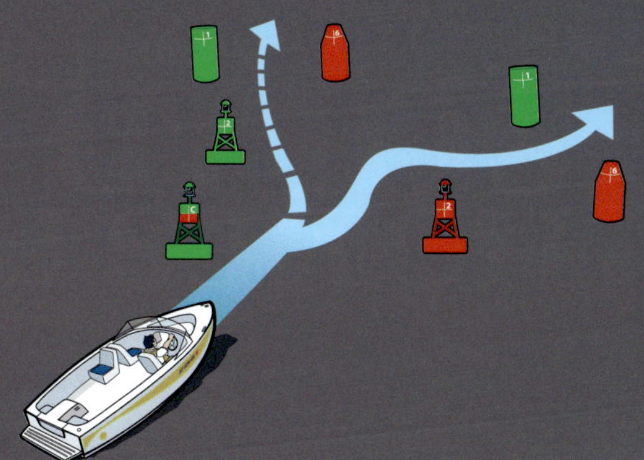

QUICK REFERENCE GUIDE

→ Navigation

→ Buoys

→ Knots

→ Pre-departure Checklist

→ Trip Plan (Sail Plan)

SECTORS OF NAVIGATION

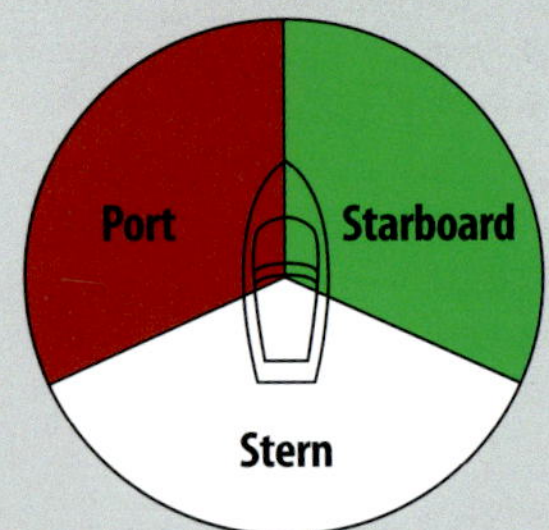

Port: If a power-driven vessel approaches within this sector, maintain with caution, your course and speed.

Starboard: If any vessel approaches within this sector, keep out of its way. *(Note: This rule may not always apply if one or both vessels are sailboats.)*

Stern: If any vessel approaches this sector, maintain with caution, your course and speed.

Rules of the Road

The rules of the road in navigation are often similar to the rules on land. The Collision Regulations contain many rules pertaining to navigation; however, four rules are basic to navigation.

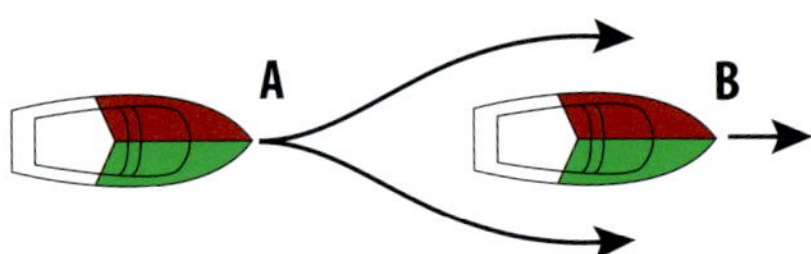

Overtaking—A boat that is overtaking another must steer clear of the overtaken vessel's path.

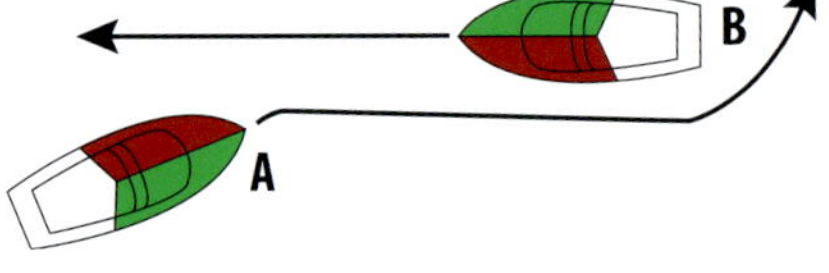

Port Approach—A vessel approaching from the port side must give way. (A) keeps clear of and must avoid crossing ahead of (B).

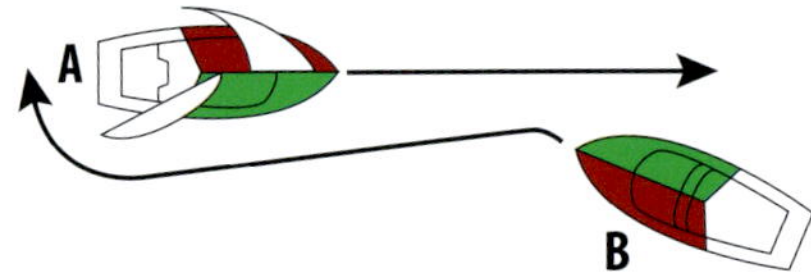

Sailboat Approach—As a general rule, rowboats, sailing vessels and canoes have the right-of-way over power- driven boats. However, if one vessel is unable to manoeuver as it normally would, the most manoeuverable vessel gives way.

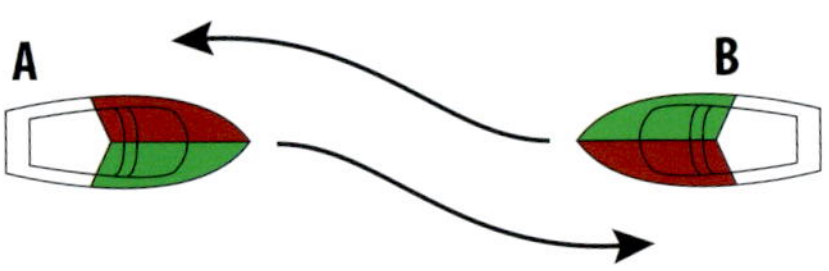

Head-on Approach—When two vessels are heading toward each other, each must reroute and pass to the right of the other. (A) blows one blast and alters course to starboard, (B) blows one blast and alters course to starboard.

BUOYS

Port-Hand Buoys
Green in colour and must be kept on the port (left) side of the vessel when going upstream.

Starboard-Hand Buoys
Red in colour and must be kept on the starboard (right) side of the vessel when going upstream.

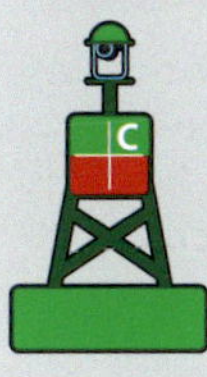

Bifurcation Buoys
Can be passed on either side in the upstream direction, with preference to the top-most band colour.

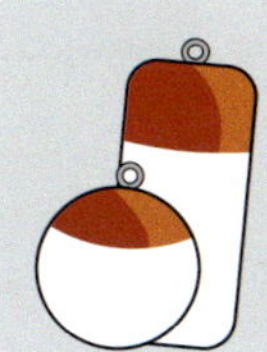

Mooring Buoys
Used to moor or secure vessels.

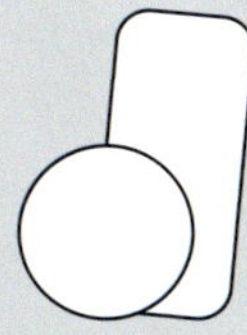

Swimming Buoys
Used to mark the perimeter of a swimming area.

Diving Buoys
Marks an area where diving activity is in progress.

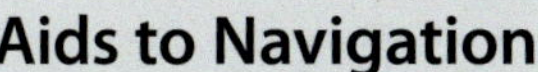

Aids to Navigation

In addition to their onboard equipment, boaters can rely on external aids to navigation. These are devices (buoys) or systems (collision regulations) which can help operators of pleasure craft determine their position and course. They also can warn of dangers or obstructions and advise operators of the best or preferred route.

RED TO THE RIGHT WHEN RETURNING

KNOTS

The Bowline Knot
Great multi-purpose knot that creates a strong and reliable loop.

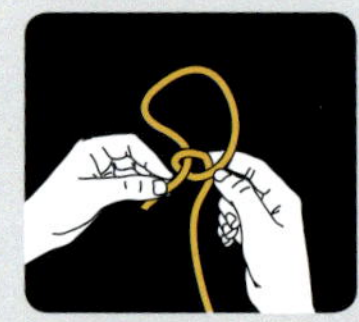
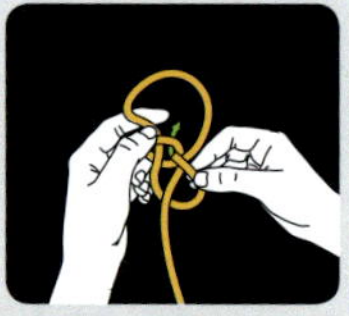
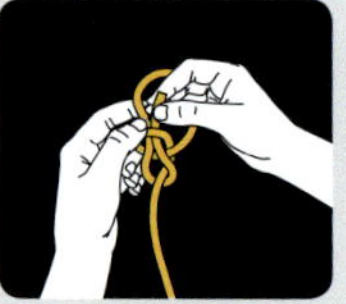

The Round Turn & Two Half Hitches
Used for securing your boat to a post or piling.

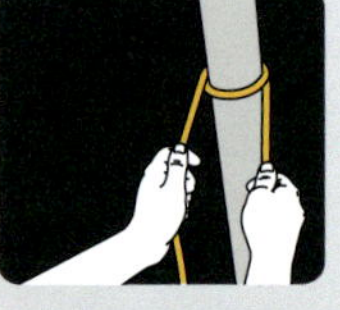

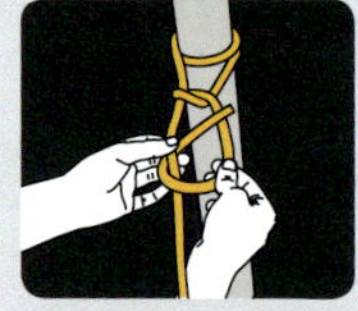
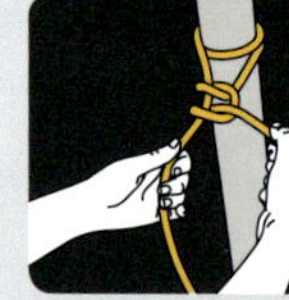

The Reef Knot (or Square Knot)
Used for tying two lines together.

The Cleat Hitch
Used for securing your boat to a cleat (on a dock or another boat).

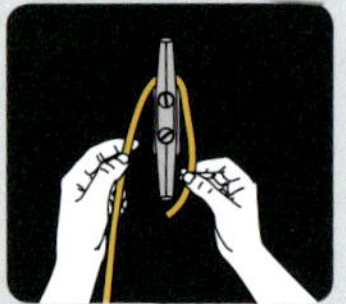
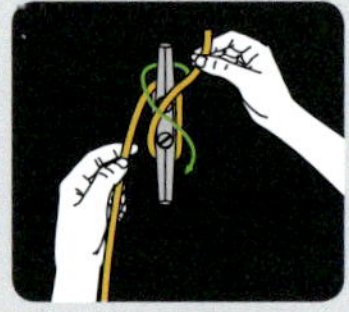
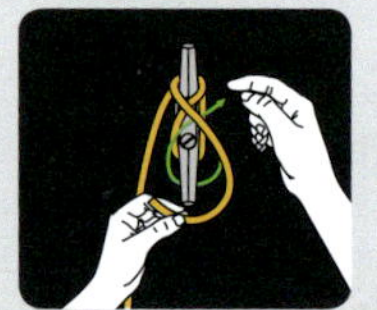
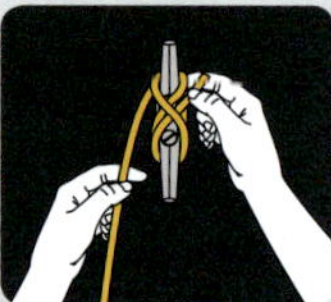

PRE-DEPARTURE CHECKLIST

Equipment

(ensure all are onboard and in working order*)

- ☐ **Personal lifesaving appliances** (eg. lifejackets, throwable devices, re-boarding device) (1 correct-sized lifejacket for each person aboard)
- ☐ **Boating safety equipment** (eg. oars, anchor, bailer, fire extinguisher)
- ☐ **Distress equipment** (eg. flares, watertight flashlight)
- ☐ **Navigation equipment** (eg. sound signaling device, lighting)
- ☐ **Repair equipment** (eg. tools, spare parts - fuel filter, light bulbs, etc.)
- ☐ **First Aid kit** (incl. dry clothes, water, emergency rations)
- ☐ **Communication equipment** (eg. VHF radio, cellphone)

**Please consult Transport Canada to verify the required equipment for your particular watercraft.*

DOWNLOAD THE CHECKLIST & TRIP PLAN (SAIL PLAN)

Inform

(ensure all passengers know the following)

- ☐ **The location of the First Aid kit**
- ☐ **The location of the distress equipment**
- ☐ **The location of the PFDs and throwable devices**
- ☐ **The location of the fire extinguishers**
- ☐ **Storm weather and falls overboard procedures**
- ☐ **Radio operations**

Documentation

(ensure the following are onboard, if applicable)

- ☐ **Pleasure Craft Operator Card**
- ☐ **Fishing / hunting licenses**
- ☐ **Radio license**
- ☐ **Local navigation charts**
- ☐ **Pleasure Craft License**

Things to do

(these must be completed before leaving)

- ☐ **Get the weather forecast**
- ☐ **Get updated charts noting hazards and marinas for the operating area**
- ☐ **Give a trip plan (sail plan) to a responsible person on shore**

Things to check

(ensure all of the following are checked)

- ☐ **Batteries are charged**
- ☐ **All fluid levels are full** (eg. antifreeze, battery, oil, transmission, coolant)
- ☐ **The drainage plug is in place**
- ☐ **Has enough fuel for the trip** (1/3 out, 1/3 back, 1/3 for reserve)
- ☐ **Hull / structural damage**
- ☐ **Oil or water leaks**

Mechanical

(ensure all are in working condition)

- ☐ **Navigation equipment**
- ☐ **Powered devices**
- ☐ **Engine & fittings**
- ☐ **Bilge pumps: manual and electric** (should be clear of debris)
- ☐ **VHF radio**
- ☐ **All hoses and belts**

TRIP PLAN (SAIL PLAN)

Information

Owner's Name:

Owner's Address:

Telephone Number:

Vessel's Name:

Vessel License Number:

Size of Vessel: | **Colour:**

Type of Vessel: ☐ **Sailboat** ☐ **Power Boat**

Hull Type: ☐ **Flat** ☐ **Round** ☐ **Deep-V Hull** ☐ **Multi-Hull**

Deck Type:

Cabin Type:

Type of Engine: ☐ **Outboard** ☐ **Inboard** ☐ **Sterndrive**

Other Distinguishing Features:

Radio Channels Monitored:

Satellite or Cellular Telephone Number(s):

Safety Equipment Onboard

Flares (Qty and Type)**:**

Life Rafts (Qty)**:** | **Lifejackets/PFDs** (Qty)**:**

Dinghy/Small Boat (inc. colour)**:**

Other:

Search and Rescue Telephone Number:

Trip Details (include these details every trip)

Date of Departure: | **Time of Departure:**

Leaving From:

Heading To:

Proposed Route:

Stop Over Point:

Est. Date/Time of Arrival:

Number of Persons Onboard:

Passenger Allergies/Illnesses (if any):

INDEX

INDEX

P-R

S-T-W